MW01128154

Stoicism for Inner Peace

Edited by Fleur Marie Vaz

ISBN: 9798725807226
Printed by Amazon Kindle Direct Publishing

First print, January 2021

www.einzelganger.co

Thank you supporters and subscribers.

— Einzelgänger

Contents

Preface

━━━━━━━━━━━ ○ƆᗰⰙᗰᗅᗰƆ○ ━━━━━━━━━━━

Stoicism was founded by Zeno of Citium in the city of Athens and is currently experiencing a revival. When I first encountered Stoic philosophy, I was surprised at how practical and timeless the core ideas of the ancient Stoics are. As if humanity had never changed, and the best and worst of human nature had stood the test of time, the countless scriptures from Greek and Roman antiquity (at least: those that have survived) provide invaluable wisdom for modern times.

Roman Emperor Marcus Aurelius, for example, saved words of wisdom which he lived by in a journal that was later published as *Meditations*. And the statesman and philosopher Lucius Annaeus Seneca left us a vast collection of philosophical letters and essays, from which *De Epistulae Morales* (Moral Letters) to his friend Lucilius are considered his most significant work. Then, we have the slave Epictetus, who became one of the greatest Stoic philosophers of all time, and whose teachings were written down by his pupil Arrian. The legacy of these three prominent Stoic philosophers, along with remnants of writings by other philosophers like Chrysippus and founder Zeno, form the resource for contemporary Stoics.

Stoicism can be practiced by us today in different degrees. Some might argue that one has to become 'a

Stoic' and live the philosophy to the smallest detail. This is a noble endeavor. But in my experience one doesn't have to follow Stoicism religiously to experience the benefits of what it teaches. The practical, rational as well as logical nature of Stoic wisdom enables us to apply it instantly to situations that cause distress, similar to placing a bandage on a wound. And, if we do this repeatedly, our reactions to life's events will transform, until we begin to apply Stoicism on autopilot as if we're carrying our philosophical first aid kit everywhere we go. Nevertheless, it's not a substitute for professional mental help where needed. I see it rather as a transformative tool that, when used consistently, can gradually change the way we perceive the world.

Before I started my YouTube channel *Einzelgänger*, I was looking for video content that converted wisdom from the old Stoic texts into present-day, easy to digest, and easy to apply wisdom. Sure, there was already plenty of good content around, but not precisely what I was looking for. See, life unfolds in different situations that evoke a plethora of different mental states in us like anger, envy, or fear, which disturb our inner peace. What I was looking for was simple, down-to-earth directions distilled from Stoic philosophy, which are tailor-made for specific situations and mental states. What to do when we're panicking? How to deal with insults? How to summon a happy mood? How to cope with financial problems?

The Stoics have answers to these enduring questions, but they're hidden and spread out across different texts and fragments that date from 300 BC. Even though Seneca's moral letters come close to my demands, I figured that we need something newer, simpler, more concise and to the point. With a master's degree in religious studies, and a modest background in publishing about religion-related subjects in magazines and newspapers, I was already used to delving into old scriptures. Thus, I decided to take on the task of selecting, compiling and adding material myself.

In a growing collection of videos, I've put Stoic wisdom in numerous different contexts, adding my commentary and interpretation to make it consumable for a present-day audience. After more than two years of producing videos and simultaneously increasing my knowledge about Stoicism, I concluded that my existing content needed revision, nuance, and expansion where needed. Hence, I made a selection of essays (in this case the ones that are concerned with inner peace) and started to improve them. I've also included several unreleased pieces as a bonus. With the help of editor Fleur Marie Vaz these overhauled scripts have been turned into this book.

Hopefully, these collected works will assist you in finding tranquility the Stoic way.

- Einzelgänger

An Introduction (the Power of Indifference)

Emperor Marcus Aurelius was the most powerful man on earth. He ruled the Roman Empire from CE161 to 180, during which time he defeated the Parthian Empire, and fought battles against fierce enemies like Germanic tribes and the Sarmatians. The Roman army that he commanded was feared in all corners of the known world. There's no question that a man of his stature had unlimited access to pleasure. He could have had his fill of pleasure with any woman he desired while being intoxicated with the best wines of the empire, until old age and death.

It's difficult to imagine absolute power. And it's probably even more difficult to handle it. Many powerful people of the past (and present) serve as proof that power corrupts, as they became slaves of their greed and hunger for more. But Marcus Aurelius sprang from a different well. Even though he was conscious of the fact that momentary pleasure was available to him in abundance, he turned away from excessive carnal pleasures, indulgent wine consumption, and the sick sadistic sequences in the colosseum where the Roman elite went for entertainment. This was in stark contrast to his son and successor Commodus, who was infamous for his cruelty, and eventually cared more for hunting and gladiators than the affairs of state.

Marcus Aurelius' memoirs are more about his determination and struggle with himself. This collection of short philosophical notes was not intended to be published and didn't even have an official title. Later, when they were published nonetheless, his work became known as *Tὰ εἰς ἑαυτόν (Ta eis heauton)*, commonly known in modern times as *Meditations*. Marcus Aurelius was among the adherents of the philosophical school named Stoicism. His *Meditations* became a key work that is widely used as a source by modern Stoics.

Let's look at some fundamental beliefs of Stoicism. The Stoics of ancient times observed that from the human perspective two categories can be distinguished: things that we *do not* control and things we *do* control. A most basic and clear explanation of this dichotomy of control can be found in the *Enchiridion*, which is a compilation of sayings by Epictetus that were written down by his pupil Arrian. Epictetus was another significant Stoic philosopher that presents us with a fundamental tenet of Stoicism, which is that most things are simply not up to us. Think about exterior things like our friends, our colleagues, our intimate partners, the economy, the number of likes on Facebook, things that politicians say, or the deterioration of our bodies. Do we actually control these things? Yes, we can influence them. But, even if we do everything right, the economy can still collapse, our money can be taken from us, and our intimate partners can cheat on us or die.

10

At the end of the day, there is nothing we can do to exclude misfortune. Adversity is an inherent part of life. This sounds depressing and pessimistic, especially for overly optimistic people that always expect things to go right. With this attitude, they leave the house cheerfully every morning, but when they get home in the afternoon there's the likelihood that reality will step in to disappoint and defeat them.

But don't worry. There are still aspects of our life that *are* up to us. Among them are the opinions we form, the decisions we make, or, simply put, our actions. What happens around us is not up to us. The position we take towards the outside world *is* up to us. Epictetus emphasizes that our focus should lie on the things within our control, while maintaining a contempt for the things not in our control.

Severe illness is not something we have control over. We can mitigate the symptoms or use healing therapies hoping that the patient recovers. But the results are not up to us. Nevertheless, the patient can decide which position they take in regards to the situation. When the sickness is fully accepted, and the possibility of death as well, a human being can reach a state of inner peace (this is not medical advice − it's philosophy). Staying calm during adversity, and letting go of the results, may come across as indifferent. However, this tranquility helps us to act in agreement with reason, instead of being overwhelmed by emotion. This probably leads to making better choices which increases the chances of recovery.

So, is Stoicism about eradicating emotion? Contrary to popular belief, this is far from true. The ability to feel deeply is part of human nature as much as the ability to think rationally. Reason can trump emotion to large extent because it allows us to choose how we handle emotion. Will we let emotions take over? Will we view them as sensations that come and go like the waves of the ocean? Or will we see them as indicators that help us to identify what's going on? The stereotype of the cold, emotionless Stoic is nonsense. Emotions are, like many things, part of human nature.

In Stoicism, nature is what it's all about. Marcus Aurelius repeatedly states that life is best lived in *accordance with* nature or "as nature requires". In this context, nature refers to the greater whole, our role in it as human beings, and our inborn nature. Stoics believe that 'virtue' is the highest good, and also follow the idea that virtue is according to nature: living virtuously is what we're designed to do. By living virtuously we'll reach *eudaimonia* (see chapter 'Happiness'). A condition for *eudaimonia* is *apatheia. Apatheia* isn't the same as the English word 'apathy:' it can be translated to 'equanimity,' or, more simply, 'inner peace.'

The practical side of Stoicism is where the fun is. Modern Stoics perform several exercises to achieve inner peace, like the *praemeditatio malorum* (negative visualization) which is a way to prepare ourselves for meeting with misfortune and, specifically, difficult people. Another one is *memento mori* (remembering death), which is the art of remembering that death is an inevitable part of life. Another exercise is called the *'view from above'* in which we see ourselves from a cosmic viewpoint. This way, we realize how small and unimportant we are compared to the vastness of the universe. There are several more exercises, and I'll explain them all in separate chapters in the last section of the book.

That indifference is power, the Stoics know very well. Life is short. That's why it's important to channel our life energy towards essential and important things and leave unimportant things be. Especially in contemporary times, Stoicism can be a valuable instrument to give our lives guidance, so we don't drown in a sea of stimuli and distractions.

Love of Fate

Excessive worry about the future causes a very undesirable experience called anxiety. This could be short-term anxiety during the day because of something you've planned in the evening, or it could be long-term anxiety about a future that is completely uncertain and out of your control. Modern Stoics have a simple but very effective trick to ease this anxiety: *amor fati.* This Latin phrase means 'love of fate.' There is tremendous power in being able to embrace whatever happens. German philosopher Friedrich Nietzsche, although he rejected Stoicism, described *amor fati* as his formula for greatness:

> *"..that one wants nothing to be different, not in the future, not in the past, not for all eternity. Not only to endure what is necessary, still less to conceal it, all idealism is falseness in the face of necessity, but to love it."*

Friedrich Nietzsche, *Dithyrambs of Dionysus* (ed. Learning Links, 1984)

Imagine that there are two versions of yourself, the anxious you and the Stoic you. Now, let's say that you work in a company that recently announced a reorganization plan. As a result, many of its employees would be laid off. This tragic news came one day after you visited your doctor, who told you that you might have a chronic illness. On top of that, the relationship with your significant other is on the rocks.

When obstacles of great significance appear in our lives, this most likely leads to drastic change. This *change* is most worrying for the anxious part of ourselves, especially because the human mind tends to judge change within a spectrum of two opposites, *desire* and *aversion*. The nature of desire and aversion is such that they set us up for emotional distress. Surely, when life changes in a desirable way, we have a pleasurable experience. Winning the lottery, for example, often leads to us becoming infatuated and temporarily residing on the proverbial cloud 9. But when life changes into a position we are averse to, like losing our money, a loved one, or ending up in prison, we'll experience pain.

Let's imagine that your life is going in an unfavorable direction. You're about to lose your job, you're struggling to pay the bills, and you're chronically ill. Now, the anxious part of you starts worrying and this keeps you up at night. You're terrorized by repetitive thoughts, like:

"Will I be laid off?"

"What am I supposed to do next?"

"What if my chronic illness hinders me from finding another job?"

"What if I can't pay my mortgage anymore?"

15

"What if my partner leaves me?"

You can influence these things in part. For the most part, though, you cannot. The underlying truth is that the future is beyond your control. The problem of the anxious part of ourselves is that it's a control freak. I can attest to that. If I'm anxious, it's mostly because I want to control the future – which is impossible. Control freaks simply cannot handle insecurity. They are stuck in the dreadful absurdity of trying to figure out what cannot be figured out, and with repetitive attempts they keep trying nonetheless. The Stoic you, however, has a different approach. It fully embraces fate *no matter what.*

Amor fati doesn't mean that we should sit in an armchair all day letting life pass by. It means that we make the best of every moment as far as fate allows it. It means that we work towards our goals, give them our all, but, when the results turn out to be different than expected, fully embrace and accept our fate. You'll keep your job? Great. Do you get laid off? Even though we can't control fate, it's still in our power to make the best of it. Moreover, who knows what opportunities will present themselves to you? Are you healthy? Great. Are you chronically ill? "Sickness is a hindrance to the body, but not to your ability to choose, unless that is your choice," Epictetus once uttered. Wouldn't it be a challenge to make your life worth living despite the fact you're sick? Many people do. And they are humanity's greatest inspirations. Your partner stays faithful? Great. Your partner cheats? Well, good riddance! This has created the opportunity to focus on yourself, which may lead to rapid personal growth, deep introspection, and the joy of solitude. Also, a more suitable person might appear in your life along the way. Who knows? Nobody can predict the future.

When we embrace whatever happens, what could go wrong? Nothing. And *amor fati* creates just that. When things can't go wrong, there's nothing to worry about. When there's nothing to worry about, the fear of the future won't sap our energy and make us feel miserable. By unconditionally embracing our destiny, we have nothing to fear.

Insults

Among other things, Stoicism teaches us how to reach a peaceful state of mind and be unmoved by things that are not up to us. One of these things is insults. Being insulted by someone often leads to the receiver getting hurt, angry, and even resentful. I've written extensively about the dynamic between insults and the insulter (and how to fortify the mind against insults) in my first book called *Unoffendable: The Art of Thriving in a World Full of Jerks*. An essential lesson in this book is reminding ourselves that what people say to us is beyond our control. Nevertheless, the majority of people seem to get triggered when insulted.

In this age of rapid communication, it seems that no matter what we say, there is always someone getting offended. It's almost like some people are deliberately looking for the experience of 'taking offense,' to let out their anger and aggressively make a point. I think that most Stoics would agree that getting triggered is mostly a waste of time. Of course, there are situations in which self-defense is a must, but something petty like a verbal insult isn't worth our time and energy. Below you'll find a relevant excerpt from *Unoffendable* about the absurdity of answering insults with violence.

There's a distinction between physical violence and insults. Physical violence harms the body. Insults, however, only harm us when we let them. Are we really going to run the risk of getting our lives ruined because someone calls us a name? "You're walking down the street and somebody calls you a name. You're gonna walk across the street, get into a fistfight, get thrown in jail, get your whole life derailed, just because someone called you a name?" says Schoenheit. Getting triggered by an insult is one thing; using violence to respond to an insult is even more stupid. Unfortunately, violence often begins with insults. I've already given the example of how insulting one's mother can lead to murder. Another recurring dynamic is soccer supporters that always begin by insulting each other before they resort to physical violence, resulting in people getting hurt, getting arrested or even killed.

The gap between insults and actual violence is often wide enough to give us room to let insults (and even threats) slide off our shoulders, and move on. This way, we maintain our peace of mind. Approaching an insult can be done in different ways, depending on the type of insult. When someone throws an insult at me, the first thing I ask myself is: "Who am I dealing with?" The insulter is often just plain ignorant. If that's indeed the case, spending time addressing these insults is kind of pointless.

One way to deal with insults is called the *praemeditatio malorum*. This Stoic form of meditation is a useful preventive measure that makes it easier for us to buttress ourselves against insults and the people who blurt them out (see chapter 'Praemeditatio Malorum'). Seneca goes one step further. He sees anger, along with insults and even physical violence, as something that should be stopped as quickly as possible to prevent further escalation. Most people would agree that the best response to a punch in the face would be 'to punch back.' But in his work *Of Anger* (that was addressed to his elder brother Novatus) he explains that 'not striking back' is *the* way to stop the quarrel. Yes, by doing so, the attacker might be perceived as the winner but, according to Seneca, the winner is the real loser. The *real* winner is the one who prevented serious damage from being inflicted, like a wound, or a broken leg. The real loser is the one who intended to provoke a reaction but didn't get what he wanted. Seneca wrote:

> *"He struck you; well then, do you fall back: if you strike him in turn you will give him both an opportunity and an excuse for striking you again; you will not be able to withdraw yourself from the struggle when you please."*

Lucius Annaeus Seneca, *Of Anger*, 2.34

Not reacting to insults doesn't mean that we shouldn't defend ourselves, if necessary. Especially when our life is in danger, striking down our enemy is necessary to survive. But when someone insults us, our lives are rarely in danger. Thus, the 'live and let live' attitude in regards to insults makes perfect sense. Believe it or not, some insults carry wisdom in them. We can use this wisdom to our advantage. When we feel offended by someone, instead of getting angry and striking back, we could take it as an opportunity for reflection.

"What can I learn from this?"

"What is my role in this?"

"Should I ask the insulter to explain more about the insult?"

"Could this be an opportunity to improve the relationship with the insulter?"

Calmly examining an insult is like killing two birds with one stone. Firstly, we maintain our peace of mind. Secondly, we're given an opportunity for improvement. When the insulter tells the truth, what's the point of getting upset about it? After all, it's the truth. Epictetus teaches us to remind ourselves that, it is not the external circumstances that create the insult, but our judgments, as is recorded in the *Enchiridion*:

> *"Remember, that not he who gives ill language or a blow insults, but the principle which represents these things as insulting. When, therefore, anyone provokes you, be assured that it is your own opinion which provokes you."*

Epictetus, *Enchiridion*, 20

21

People that are offended by petty things often don't realize that their minds have turned this pettiness into insults. Many times, they are offended by people that don't even intend to be insulting. In that case, it might be a good idea to examine our minds before we get triggered. What is my frame of reference? What's my relationship to this matter? What preconceptions do I have?

Some people stay angry for days – some even for years. When gravely insulted, one feels justified in being angry. But petty insults, even those that weren't meant as insults, could provoke some people just as much. And this resentment oftentimes goes together with a desire for revenge. This can lead to even more suffering than the event itself. So, isn't it much better to just let it go?

Letting go seems hard. A good way to learn how this is done is by looking at animals. Animals fight and quarrel, and a few minutes later resume their customary posture, wagging their tails as if nothing happened. Like Stoics, they live in the present moment, not holding on to resentment as humans do. The world isn't perfect, and we're not entitled to a perfect life, no matter if the media tells you otherwise. Many things in life, especially people, will act in ways that are *not* in your best interests. What people throw in your direction is not up to you. Getting offended, however, is a choice. If we let go of the nastiness that people throw at us, we'll travel lightly through life, so we can spend our energy on things that truly matter.

Happiness

Many people these days are concerned with achieving happiness in life, but often lack the skills and knowledge to do so. Luckily, thousands of years ago, the old Stoics had already figured out how to suffer less and enjoy more. How? With a system of exercises, wisdom, and ethics inspired by the benevolence of the universe, Stoicism is a philosophy for happiness. However, it's important to notice that the meaning of the word 'happiness' is different for every person. Some people think of happiness as having a lot of money. Other people think about enjoying the company of their loved ones. To Stoics, the ultimate happiness is *eudaimonia*. This Greek word can be translated into 'a state of flourishing' which also entails a sense of inner peace and tranquility.

The following paragraphs contain three 'portals' to Stoic happiness that we can access by changing the way we think.

1)   The portal of (right) judgment

The Stoics believed that events aren't inherently good or bad, but that the mind makes them so. Why is this important? Because most things that happen in our lives are beyond our control, so there are very few things over which we *do* have control. Among the things that are within our control is our opinion or, in other words, our ability to judge. An ancient Greek or Roman person regularly went for a nice bath in one of the many bathhouses. During these visits, things like theft, splashing water, and people using abusive language were not uncommon. These may seem undesirable experiences but, according to Stoic thought, the way these experiences affect us depends on how we judge them. Let's give Epictetus a moment to share his thoughts:

> *"For thus, if any hindrance arises in bathing, you will have it ready to say: 'It was not only to bathe that I desired, but to keep my mind in a state conformable to nature; and I will not keep it if I am bothered at things that happen.'"*

Epictetus, *Enchiridion*, 4

2) The portal of virtue

As mentioned earlier, Stoic happiness equals living in accordance with nature which, in turn, equals living virtuously. "Virtue is according to nature; vice is opposed to it and hostile," Seneca wrote in his fiftieth letter to Lucilius. The terms 'virtue' and 'nature' may sound vague, but the Stoics have an ethical system that explains how 'virtuous living' is conducted. First of all, they discern between virtue and vice. Virtues are considered 'good' and go along *with* nature. Vices are considered 'bad' and go *against* nature. Virtue can be subdivided into *wisdom, justice, courage, and moderation* (which are the cardinal virtues). Vice can be subdivided into *foolishness, injustice, cowardice, and intemperance.* According to the Stoics, virtue leads to happiness and vice leads to misery. Hence, the solution for a happy life is to live virtuously and avoid vice. Sounds simple, right?

Of course, there's a lot more to life than good and bad. In the large gray area between the favorable zenith of virtue and the undesirable nadir of vice are the 'indifferents' (yes, it's a noun). The Stoics further distinguish 'preferred indifferents' and 'dispreferred indifferents.' Examples of preferred indifferents are strength, wealth, pleasure, and a good reputation. These attributes are positive in regards to our natural condition but don't necessarily lead to happiness. Examples of dispreferred indifferents are disease, weakness, ugliness, poverty, and low reputation. These attributes are negative in regards to our natural condition but don't necessarily lead to misery. Indifferents aren't necessarily good or bad but, rather, preferred or dispreferred. Because preferred indifferents are seen as inferior to virtue and fundamentally beyond our control, they shouldn't be the focus when one wishes to be happy.

Nevertheless, creating favorable circumstances could help us with increasing virtue, and less favorable circumstances could facilitate vice. But, regardless of what circumstances we live in, the right path is always accessible. The fact that Epictetus the slave and Marcus Aurelius the emperor both practiced Stoicism proves that the amount of money you have or the social status you enjoy, are ultimately not the deciding factors when it comes to virtuous living.

3) The portal of (low) expectations

The essence of high expectations is that we expect a desirable outcome in regards to things we do not have control over. Taking such a position towards external things will, eventually, lead to disappointment, because they don't often work out the way we ourselves imagined. For example, you might expect your father to act in a certain way: like a 'good' father, who's there for you when you need him, respects your decisions, and shows you affection. But instead, he's flaky, doesn't respect your decisions at all, and acts cold and without affection. Epictetus argues that it's not the nature of the father that hurts us, but the expectations we have of our fathers.

"Are you naturally entitled, then, to a good father? No, only to a father."

Epictetus, *Enchiridion*, 30

Epictetus points out that you're not entitled to the things you wish for, but only to the things that are naturally given to you. What Fortune (which refers to the ancient Greek deity Fortuna, the goddess of chance, luck and fate) does is not ours to decide. Thus, when our expectations exceed what nature ultimately has in store for us, we suffer. This suffering comes from wanting things to happen differently and not from the events themselves. Unfortunately, we're not entitled to anything. Some people die young, while others live beyond the age of hundred years. Many people never become rich (despite their efforts) while others are fed with a golden spoon. Even though we can influence our destiny, the Stoics teach us that it's ultimately out of our control.

Lowering our expectations will make adversity more bearable and good fortune more enjoyable. We can lower not only our expectations for life in the long term, but the smaller daily occurrences as well, like dealing with other people. As emperor, Marcus Aurelius had to deal with many difficult people and knew that a too optimistic outlook would only set him up for disappointment. Hence, in the morning, he premeditated on the undesirable things that could happen when he was out doing his business, so that he wouldn't start his day with false expectations (see chapter 'Praemeditatio Malorum').

What Others Think

"It never ceases to amaze me: we all love ourselves more than other people, but care more about their opinion than our own."

Marcus Aurelius, *Meditations*, 12.4

Marcus Aurelius was right when he said that we care more about people's opinions than our own. People spend so much energy worrying about what other people think about them. This is a huge waste of time; especially in our age of individualism. There's no doubt that it's very easy to get caught up in this ongoing collective worry about people's opinions: even if we don't know them! But why do we engage in such behavior?

Our desire to be liked probably comes from the deeply rooted fear of being abandoned. In the past, especially during the tribal age, abandonment could easily mean death, so being liked was useful for survival. We can see this in animals, too. Dogs, for example, are naturally herd creatures and dread to be left alone, so they cry and moan when their owner leaves the house. But, when we logically look at this, the need for company is contextual. It's scientifically proven that infants need adult caretakers to survive and grow up. Sick and elderly people most likely (will) need the help of their fellow human beings to survive as well. But in the current

29

modern world, most of us are not in danger when other people simply don't like or disapprove of us, unless, perhaps, we mess with the wrong person or break the law. Sure, it would be preferable to be loved by our surroundings than to receive a bunch of likes and views on YouTube. We certainly don't need all this approval and validation to be happy, let alone survive.

As the Stoics would say: a good reputation is a preferred indifferent (see chapter 'Happiness'). Reputation is nice to have, but if we don't, it doesn't exclude virtuous living and the happiness that comes with that. Moreover, Epictetus mentioned that, when we choose the path of (Stoic) philosophy, we must be prepared to be ridiculed and not be swayed by it.

> *"If you have an earnest desire of attaining to philosophy, prepare yourself from the very first to be laughed at, to be sneered by the multitude, to hear them say, 'He is returned to us a philosopher all at once,' and 'Whence this supercilious look?' Now, for your part, don't have a supercilious look indeed; but keep steadily to those things which appear best to you as one appointed by God to this station. For remember that, if you adhere to the same point, those very persons who at first ridiculed will afterwards admire you. But if you are conquered by them, you will incur a double ridicule."*

If you live well, why should you care about what others think? You know that *you* live well and that's what counts. Wasn't Jesus Christ despised by the masses even though He embodied the good? What's more important: people's validation or living a good life? A great reputation or being happy and content? When we look at the very nature of receiving validation – from a physical audience clapping to likes on Facebook – what do we see? It's nothing more than a few bodily movements and some pixels on a screen that give us a temporary rush of pleasure. Despite the meaninglessness of it, people still crave it so much. We even see people getting upset when they don't receive the validation they think they deserve, or when they find out that someone dislikes them or even hates them. In some cases, a simple and meaningless insult leads to violence.

The Stoics pointed out long ago that we do not control the opinions of others, and that the things we do not control are fickle. The more we value things beyond our control, the less control we have. Let's face it. No matter how much we try, there'll always be people that don't like us. There'll always be people that are ungrateful, hostile, hateful, mean, and judgmental. When we don't accept that such people are part of life, we're prone to becoming resentful, and sometimes spend a lifetime pondering over the nasty things they say.

"When another blames you or hates you, or when men say anything injurious about you, approach their poor souls, penetrate within, and see what kind of men they are. You will discover that there is no reason to be concerned that these men have this or that opinion about you."

Marcus Aurelius, *Meditations*, 9.27

Resentment is like drinking poison and waiting for the other person to die: it's a waste of time. With a little bit of compassion, we'll see that those who offend us are human beings after all. There are many possible reasons *why* they think what they think, and say what they say. It may be ignorance, bias, frustration, or they might be pointing out something that's truly deficient about us. If the latter is the case, we have the option to fix it or let it be. In some cases, it's not unwise to be 'concerned' about other people's opinions if the criticism is helpful in any way. However, ruminating about someone else's dislike towards us won't get us anywhere. Even though we're powerless in regards to what other people think, how we handle it is definitely within our power. Being hurt by other people's opinions isn't caused by *them*; it's caused by our minds worrying about things that are outside us and irrelevant to our mental well-being. And at the end of the day, what other people think is none of our business.

Love & Lust

You might be wondering how the ancient Stoics viewed love and lust. Were they hopeless romantics or rather cold and distant? Were they pleasure-seekers enjoying polyamory or did they value the duties of marriage? There's a big difference between love and lust, although in today's day and age there seems to be little distinction. We could say that unconditional love is the purest form of love there is and something that lies within our control. Epictetus described the things in our control as "by nature free, unrestrained, and unhindered." That's why we can give this type of love away freely, and don't need anything in return; so the quality of it doesn't depend on what outside forces are up to. Lust, on the other hand, is a desire for something that is *not* in our control. When we're lustful, we crave the body of another human being. And when this body, for some reason, isn't available, we suffer. Epictetus described the things not in our control as "weak, slavish, restrained, belonging to others."

Living in a Western culture I see a great emphasis on 'romantic love.' The romantic love ideal has become such an important pursuit that we have elevated it to the level of an 'ultimate concern.' More often than not (especially in Western secularized countries), romantic love rises above any form of religion and spirituality. Some people *live* for romance, making this mesmerizing experience the focus of their lives. Unfortunately, there's a problem with this pursuit. When two people fall in love, they reside in a period of infatuation popularly called the 'honeymoon phase.' Whether or not nature meant this to be simply an incentive to procreate, the honeymoon phase doesn't last. After the intense euphoria decreases, it's not unlikely that people start to feel cheated. Without the rose-colored glasses, they see the object of their affection with, probably, the many flaws they initially overlooked. As a result, they might seek the next romantic high, and abandon 'lovers' that aren't doing it for them anymore. Such love is self-serving, rather than serving others. In many ways, romantic love is built on clinging and aversion. We cling to someone tenaciously and are averse to the idea of being separated. "He who fails to obtain the object of his desire is disappointed, and he who incurs the object of his aversion wretched," said Epictetus.

The experience of being wretched is commonly seen in individuals in a state of romantic love, in the form of 'jealousy' (see more in chapter 'Jealousy'). Such jealousy between lovers can be quite destructive: it's a fear-based emotion that a lover will leave for someone else. This often results in possessiveness, the need to control the movements of another human being to assure ourselves that they won't do things we don't like. This is just another form of clinging. Such relationships don't seem very virtuous, nor do they lead to inner peace. Still, as opposed to what some might think, the Stoics did *not* disapprove of relationships. Yet, they did not recommend clinging relationships or indulgence in lust. Seneca, for example, saw (an ongoing) indulgence in lust as the worst of all sins:

> *"But among the worst I count also those who have time for nothing but wine and lust; for none have more shameful engrossments."*

Lucius Annaeus Seneca, *On The Shortness Of Life*, 7.1

Seneca stated that those who are abandoned to the belly and lust, bear the stain of dishonor, and thought that people who are quickly angered, greedy and violent at least sin in a more "manly" fashion (as he called it). This doesn't mean that we shouldn't experience lust at all. The joy of sexual intimacy, for example, can be seen as a preferred indifferent (see chapter 'Happiness') which, according to Stoic ethics, must not be prioritized above virtuous living, which includes self-control and modesty. Intemperance is a vice. Interestingly enough, the Stoic attitude towards pleasure resembles the 'lustful appetites' in the biblical Christian tradition: *gluttony (gula)*, *fornication (luxuria)*, and *greed (avaritia)*. These are part of the lusts of the flesh.

As opposed to lustful indulgence, Seneca respected love and meaningful relationships with other people. They concerned him a great deal. He valued marriage and the duties involved and expressed his dislike of divorce and adultery. Such a stance is congruent with Stoic ethics, which upholds living a virtuous life above everything else. Stoic philosopher Musonius Rufus also valued marriage and saw mutual caring as the cornerstone of a successful union:

> *"In marriage there must be complete companionship and concern for each other on the part of both husband and wife, in health and in sickness and at all times, because they entered upon the marriage for this reason as well as to produce offspring."*

Musonius Rufus, *Lecture XIII A*

Musonius also observed that, when in a marriage people only look to their interests and neglect their partners, it is doomed to fail. We can see this happening in some affectionless marriages in which people share a roof while perpetually seeking pleasure outside the house. Musonius called this an *"existence worse than loneliness."*

For the sake of simplicity, I would say that the core of Stoic love is the facilitation of virtue. A union between two people in marriage can be seen as a potential vessel for 'good,' like caring for one another and raising children. This idea echoes through religions like Christianity and Islam, in which marriage is also seen as the correct way for two people to practice love as well as lust. Having read the ancient Stoic texts, I would say that Stoics do not disapprove of intimacy as long it doesn't impede virtue and we're realistic about our expectations. Quite harshly, Epictetus argued that we must remember the nature of the things we deeply love and be guided by this thought: "If you kiss your child, or your wife, say that you only kiss things which are human, and thus you will not be disturbed if either of them dies." Our loved ones are human and, therefore, predestined to die. Also, humans don't always do what we want them to do. If your wife cheats or your husband falls in love with a colleague, then this is also to be expected.

Breakups

⊸⧓⧓⊶⊷⊷⊷⊷ ⊷⊷⊶⧓⧓⊸

A breakup can be excruciatingly painful. But why is this the case? Without a doubt, the concept of love and romance has changed over the centuries. In all probability, there wasn't a dating culture in ancient Greece similar to what we have now. But even though civilization makes leaps and bounds forward, our physiology isn't very different from what it was 2500 years ago. We just have to read the ancient Stoics to discover that they dealt with the same emotions then as we do now: lust, craving, attachment, and anger. Stoicism suggests that such negative emotional states are either consequences of wrong ways of thinking and can be reduced by changing the way we think.

When it comes to grieving over a breakup, we could say from a Stoic perspective, that this is the result of wrong thinking and wrong pursuit. We become attached to another person, and derive our happiness (partly) from being with this person, which led to strong desires and aversions. In most cases, the attachment to this person has become so strong that a strong emotional reaction to a breakup has become inevitable – so there's nothing to beat ourselves up over. But Stoic philosophy can work as a bandage to the wound as well as provide some valuable wisdom in regards to future romantic pursuits.

To understand why we suffer so much after a breakup, we need to deconstruct what's happening with us when we break up and why we feel so bad. Needless to say, falling in love is a very intense experience. When in love, our bodies produce chemicals that make us feel euphoric, and, at some point, the only person that we can think about is the one we're in love with. All these sensations are a result of a chemical reaction by the body that we don't have control over: they overcome us. The purpose of these sensations is probably to stimulate bonding and reproduction. For some reason, we're wired in such a way that after the 'honeymoon phase' these intense feelings begin to subside and we stop idolizing the other person. But after this temporary high is gone, a deep attachment often remains.

Is attachment due to romance wrong in itself? I wouldn't say it's wrong in a moral sense, but it's the root cause of suffering. When we've gone down the rabbit hole of romantic love, we'll have to pay the price to get out of it sooner or later. It's a matter of cause and effect. When we experience a painful breakup, we're dealing with the consequences of being separated from what we're deeply attached to. Now the question arises: can we do something about it? Well, this is where the power of the rational mind comes in, which the Stoics are masters at. Even though we can't just make the pain go away magically, it's possible to change certain beliefs to accept the reality of the breakup and find a sense of peace in it.

I would now like to briefly discuss some of these beliefs, and what the Stoics say about them.

1) I need that person to be happy.

This attachment can manifest itself in clingy behavior and the illusion that we need this particular person to be happy. A common answer to this problem is that "there're plenty of fish in the sea." Although this sounds a bit cheesy, it's true. With so many people on this planet, it's insane to think that there's only one person suited to you. But, this doesn't solve the problem because, regardless of how many fish there are swimming in the sea, the fish are still something external and beyond our control. There are no guarantees that we can obtain any of these fish, even when there are plenty of them. And there are no guarantees that the fish we catch will stick around.

If we suffer from a breakup because we believe that we need the other person to be happy, we erroneously think that our happiness depends on something external. The ancient Stoics would have firmly disagreed with this! Virtue is the only thing we need to be happy from the Stoic view. Living a virtuous life is completely within our control, and doesn't necessarily include a partner. Stoics see romance, relationships, marriage, and even having a family as nonessential for happiness; they are also in the list of unreliable factors. Those things are preferred

40

indifferents (see chapter 'Happiness'): nice to have but not mandatory for a happy life.

2) I'm entitled to that person.

Feeling entitled to someone can evoke a lot of anger in people. It may lead to seeing the other person as your possession or, at least, a factor in life that we're qualified to have and that right shouldn't be taken away from us. This possessiveness often goes hand in hand with jealousy, which is a fear of losing what we have to someone else (see next section 'Jealousy'). Thus, when the person we love decides to break up with us, we feel wronged. We think that the reason for the breakup is, in some way, *unjust*. In the case of divorce, we might particularly feel betrayed as our ex-spouse breaks the promise of staying together "until death do us part," not to speak about a divorce in which cheating is involved which makes us feel even more betrayed.

At the same time, it's important to always remember that monogamy and sexual exclusivity haven't always been the norm. These concepts have become part of our normative framework over the years, as part of the culture and religious traditions – which is why many consider marriage sacred. Of course, this normativity feeds our sense of entitlement. However, in today's day and age with ever-increasing sexual freedom worldwide, dating apps, and the decline of the sanctity of marriage,

41

chances are high that relationships fall apart. Breakups have become more and more common. And so has infidelity. Stoic philosopher Epictetus had more wise words to say when it comes to positioning ourselves toward losing the things we love.

> *"Never say of anything, 'I have lost it'; but, 'I have returned it.' Is your child dead? It is returned. Is your wife dead? She is returned. Is your estate taken away? Well, and is not that likewise returned? 'But he who took it away is a bad man.' What difference is it to you who the giver assigns to take it back? While he gives it to you to possess, take care of it; but don't view it as your own, just as travelers view a hotel."*

Epictetus, *Enchiridion*, 11

This attitude might come in handy for people that worry about their partners cheating in the future. If that happens, remember that this isn't a loss. It's just a "return".

3) I'll never get over that person.

The excruciating pain that often goes together with a breakup makes it seem almost impossible to get over it. But the cliché is true: time heals all wounds. As Stoic philosopher and ancient Roman emperor Marcus Aurelius puts it:

42

"Some things are rushing into existence, others out of it. Some of what now exists is already gone. Change and flux constantly remake the world, just as the incessant progression of time remakes eternity."

Marcus Aurelius, *Meditations*, 6.15

Now, breakup pain is something we can work with. Fighting it won't help. Instead, it's better to acknowledge that it's present. Sadly, some people apply terrible coping mechanisms. I used to drink a lot of alcohol and used other mind-altering substances to cope with breakup grief, which eventually led to hangovers, increased sadness, and doing very stupid things. These were just quick fixes that wouldn't help in the long run. On top of that, I've often isolated myself after a breakup, which, in retrospect, is good in moderation and without intoxication. From my personal experience, I can say the ideal way to deal with grief is a balance of active engagement with the world and moments in solitude to 'sit with it.' The latter is important as it's embracing the reality (*amor fati*), and simply enduring the detachment phase, which can be a slow process that can take months or even years.

To learn more about how the ancient Stoics viewed immediate grief after an unfortunate event, we might want to turn to Seneca. Seneca wasn't just a Stoic

43

philosopher; he was also a statesman who held a position of power in the Roman Empire until he was charged with adultery with the emperor's sister. Exiled to Corsica, he writes to his mother these consoling words as she mourned his absence.

> *"I knew that I must not oppose your grief during its first transports, lest my very attempts at consolation might irritate it, and add fuel to it: for in diseases, also, there is nothing more hurtful than medicine applied too soon. I waited, therefore, until it exhausted itself by its own violence, and being weakened by time, so that it was able to bear remedies, would allow itself to be handled and touched."*

Seneca, *Of Consolation: To Helvia*, 1

This is my take-away from this passage: let the tears flow; be human first, and when the initial shock subsides, let's see if Stoic philosophy can be applied as a bandage to the wound.

Jealousy

When there's someone or something we cherish – like a spouse or a friend or, perhaps, a certain social status – we might experience a fear of losing that particular person or thing to someone else. This is jealousy. There's a difference between jealousy and envy. Jealousy comes from a fear of losing something to another person (which is very common in intimate relationships). Envy is wanting something that someone else has, like a car, a house, looks, and feeling discontent about not having these things ourselves. I'll talk about envy later.

When we look at jealousy from a Stoic viewpoint, we can identify two elements: *the illusion of permanence* and *the belief that external things will make us happy*. The Stoics noticed that the nature of the universe is impermanent. Nothing outside our faculties lies within our control. When we're jealous, we don't want to lose something external that we attach ourselves to. The truth is, however, that no matter how infatuated we are with our spouses, our lovers, or what not: someday we'll get separated from what we're attached to.

> *"Bear in mind that everything that exists is already fraying at the edges, and in transition, subject to fragmentation and to rot."*

Marcus Aurelius, *Meditations*, 10.18

Epictetus once pointed out that we shouldn't view external things as our own. Ownership is just an idea. It's an illusion. In reality, we can never truly own something that is beyond our control. If we could, then nothing in the world would be able to separate us from what's ours. We don't even own our bodies. If we owned them, we'd control them. We could prevent them from becoming sick and from aging, but we can't. Instead, as with anything in our lives, we borrow our bodies and they shall be returned when the time is ripe.

No matter how much effort we put into our relationships, how well our properties are secured, how great our reputation is, the truth is we can still lose the things we are attached to in the blink of an eye. The possibility of loss is not irrational, because the occurrence of loss aligns with the nature of the universe. Fear comes from resisting this occurrence. Our spouse may very well cheat on us with a co-worker tomorrow. Our supposed best friends may prefer the presence of someone else over us. These possibilities are realistic and common. Worrying about them won't stop them from happening. Trying to control the external world that's not up to us anyway is a waste of time. "But I need this person to be happy!" you say? This is not true. People loving us is a preferred indifferent (see chapter 'Happiness'). This means that it's nice to have such people in our lives and they might support us in living virtuously but, according to Stoic ethics, they're not a requirement to be happy.

Jealousy generates pain. Furthermore, we lose the things that we fear to lose anyway. If we realize that happiness isn't found in those things we're afraid to lose but rather in our ability to be content without them, we might have an easier time letting them go. Stoicism focuses on living well regardless of the circumstances. Paradoxically, when we focus on living well instead of anxiously clinging to the things that we don't want to lose, we might even attract more preferred indifferents into our lives and the ones that are already with us are more likely to stick. Being jealous only drives them away.

Envy

By narrowing down the emotion of envy, we discover that it is a form of desire, specifically directed at things that belong to other people. Desire means that we want to reach out for something that we consider as desirable, and thus, something we want for ourselves. When the thing that causes our envy is something external, like someone else's money, partner, car, or job, we desire pleasure rather than happiness. It seems that we most desire objects or people outside of ourselves. If we follow Stoic thought, we can intentionally devalue the thing we desire, as things of such nature are not reliable sources of happiness. Hence, the Stoics discourage us from making the pursuit of them our focus.

On the other hand, when it's an internal quality that makes us envious like the virtuous actions of another person or their inner peace and happiness, it might be a positive thing. We're able to see the good qualities of other people that we are lacking, which is a sign of self-reflection and an opportunity to work on ourselves. Paradoxically, when we pursue virtue and strengthen our faculties, we're likely to get rid of envy altogether. As Epictetus stated:

> *"You may be unconquerable, if you enter into no combat in which it is not in your own control to*

48

conquer. When, therefore, you see anyone eminent in honors, or power, or in high esteem on any other account, take heed not to be hurried away with the appearance, and to pronounce him happy; for, if the essence of good consists in things in our own control, there will be no room for envy or emulation."

Epictetus, *Enchiridion*, 19

Unfortunately, some people are so envious that they engage in immoral behavior like stealing, infidelity, and even murder. In the *Old Testament* and the *Quran,* there's a story about the rivalry between the brothers Cain and Abel, sons of Adam and Eve. Cain was a farmer and Abel was a shepherd. Cain offered God a part of his crops while Abel offered God the firstlings of his flock. Cain murdered his brother after God accepted Abel's offerings while He rejected his. The story doesn't explicitly mention 'envy,' but interpretations of it magnify the theme of envious rivalry between siblings, a phenomenon that's affected humankind to this day. The ancient scriptures don't mention why exactly God did this, either. One possibility is that Abel acted more virtuously by giving God the best of his flock as well as blood offerings, while Cain's offerings were of lesser quality. Another possibility could be (and many Christians would disagree) that God was acting capriciously when treating Cain and

Abel differently for no reason. Both scenarios are great starting points to look at envy from a Stoic point of view, as we can use them as metaphors for dealing with envy in everyday life.

The first scenario is that Abel indeed acted in a more virtuous way and was, therefore, rewarded by God. In this case, we can see the blood offering by Abel as a metaphor for – what the Stoics would call – an act of virtue. According to the Stoics, virtue leads to *eudaimonia* (see chapter 'Happiness'). Thus we could say that Cain was envious of Abel's virtue and the consequences of that virtue. This doesn't make Cain's envy destructive per se. At least, not yet. The problem is, however, that many envious people seek to destroy what causes their envy instead of using envy as a compass to improve *themselves.* Instead of killing his brother, Cain could have used the spark of envy to realize that Abel was doing a better job than him. He could have seen his brother as an inspiration for becoming more virtuous himself.

The second scenario is that God denied Cain's offerings for no reason, which would resemble the view of the universe in the Epicurean as well as the Absurdist sense, namely, that of randomness. Why, for example, are some born into rich families and others into poverty? Again, some people are gifted with great intelligence, others are mentally disabled. Whether or not we're all part of a divine plan, the acute sense of unfairness angered Cain so much, that he decided to act out. If Seneca was around at that time, he could have told Cain that the unfairness of life doesn't necessarily influence the ability to be happy:

> *"Come now, contrast a good man who is rolling in wealth with a man who has nothing, except that in himself he has all things; they will be equally good, though they experience unequal fortune. This same standard, as I have remarked, is to be applied to things as well as to men; virtue is just as praiseworthy if it dwells in a sound and free body, as in one which is sickly or in bondage."*

Lucius Annaeus Seneca, *Moral Letters to Lucilius*, 66.22

So, is envy a bad thing? It depends on what makes us envious of and how we deal with this emotion. From a Stoic viewpoint, being envious because of external factors like money, beauty, or the neighbor's car is unworthy of our energy. Sure, it's probably more comfortable to live in a six-bedroom villa with three BMWs in the garage than in a studio flat owning a bicycle. But, not having all these material riches that we're perpetually being sold, won't obstruct our ability to be happy. On the other hand, we can use envy as a tool to better ourselves. Looking at other people's goodness can inspire us to do good ourselves. And, even though the ancient Stoics didn't encourage the pursuit of material wealth, it's even possible to use envy as fuel to make achievements in material things as well. Overall, envy can be used as an incentive for building something great, whether it's a business, a sports career, or perhaps a creative pursuit. All of this is much better than letting envy become a tool of destruction.

That's why awareness is a key factor when dealing with envy. We might want to reflect on these questions: Why am I envious? Is my envy justified (*in other words:* does the thing I desire truly lead to happiness)? Can I use my envy to better myself and subsequently get rid of envy? The rule of thumb is that, if we just focus on our path, stop feeling entitled to the blessings of others, and be grateful for what we have, there's no reason to be envious of anything.

Aversion and Desire

The dynamics of aversion and desire lies at the base of Stoic thought when it comes to relating to the world around us. When we are averse to something, it means that we bear a strong dislike and disclination towards it. Even though it may seem harmless, aversion can cause a lot of trouble: the root of hate and fear lies in it. To understand aversion, we have to understand its polar opposite as well, which is desire. Desire breeds aversion and aversion breeds desire. We can throw in a bit of Taoist philosophy by arguing that one opposite cannot exist without the other and that both turn around a spindle. Let's say that we crave a million dollars. This strong desire automatically contains the aversion to *not* having a million dollars (which we could translate into aversion to living in poverty). By taking this position, we make our future happiness conditional: if we're able to obtain a million dollars, we'll be happy; but if we fail, we'll be miserable. Epictetus had the following to say about this mechanism:

> *"Remember that following desire promises the attainment of that of which you are desirous; and aversion promises the avoiding that to which you are averse. However, he who fails to obtain the*

object of his desire is disappointed, and he who
incurs the object of his aversion wretched."

Epictetus, *Enchiridion*, 2

Does this mean that we should abolish desire and aversion altogether? No, that would be too simplistic. The Stoics of old recognized that humans are naturally inclined towards self-preservation. We tend to desire things that are good for us and to be averse to things that aren't. This phenomenon was called *oikeiosis*. These things aren't necessary to be happy, but are good for us nonetheless, and there's no problem in desiring them. *Oikeiosis* also means a natural aversion to things that aren't good for us, like death and sickness. There's a problem, however, when these feelings of desire and aversion are too strong. But the Stoics have a solution for that.

A key element of Stoic philosophy is the virtue of moderation. In this case, moderation means that we ought to relate to the external world with temperance. Thus, inclining towards what's good for us and avoiding what isn't good for us in a moderate fashion would be ideal. So when doing so, it's always important to regulate our aversions and desires. Epictetus compared this to attending a dinner party.

"Remember that you must behave in life as at a
dinner party. Is anything brought around to you?

Put out your hand and take your share with moderation. Does it pass by you? Don't stop it. Is it not yet come? Don't stretch your desire towards it, but wait till it reaches you."

Epictetus, *Enchiridion*, 15

We don't control our circumstances, so encountering misfortune someday is to be expected. Nobody likes to be sick, but sickness is unavoidable. Nobody likes losing a loved one, but this, too, is part of life. Strong aversion leads to our environment dictating our emotions all the time. By weakening our aversions, we'll be less shaken when bad things happen to us. We can do this, for example, by consciously embracing fate, by reminding ourselves that encountering adversity is inevitable and that not incurring these things isn't the main goal, but maintaining our tranquility is.

Letting Go

Life can be extremely stressful at times. This is basically because we're holding on to illusions of control and because our minds are overthinking and ruminating round the clock. In most cases, holding on to things is a waste of energy, and overdoing it can cause mental and even physical pain. The following essay derives three ways of letting go from Stoic philosophy.

1) Becoming aware of indifferents

In the Stoic system of virtue, vice and so-called indifferents, what most people seem to hold on to are preferred indifferents (see chapter 'Happiness'). The 'indifference' associated with these things already indicates that they aren't worth so much concern. A huge television screen, a chunk of savings, or a sailboat won't lead to happiness, and not having these things won't obstruct our ability to be happy either – unlike the basic necessities of life like nutrition, water, and oxygen. I've lost count of the poor people I've met when traveling in Indonesia with smiles on their faces, and the many rich people I've encountered that are perpetually dissatisfied. This says a lot to me. In regards to the ancient Stoic texts, Seneca has some wise words to say:

"Whoever has largely surrendered himself to the power of Fortune has made for himself a huge web of disquietude, from which he cannot get free; if one would win a way to safety, there is but one road – to despise externals and to be contented with that which is honourable. For those who regard anything as better than virtue, or believe that there is any good except virtue, are spreading their arms to gather in that which Fortune tosses abroad, and are anxiously awaiting her favours."

Lucius Annaeus Seneca, *Moral Letters to Lucilius*, 74.5

The above quote is from a letter from Seneca to his friend Lucilius. In that same letter, he emphasizes that the mere grasping for externals will never get you the things that you've imagined to get in the first place. The joy of externals is always temporary. Moreover, greedy hands often end up with nothing but frustration. If we know that, at the end of the day, preferred indifferents are simply overrated and that we can still be happy with just the bare necessities, we might stop chasing them so much (or at least loosen our grip on them) as we know that not having these things isn't the end of the world. Now isn't that a calming thought?

2) Remembering impermanence

The world is completely out of control. Life comes, life goes. Empires rise, empires fall. And it's just a matter of time that planet earth vanishes because the Sun swallows it. The house we live in, the money we have in the bank, the people we love, they're all going down the drain someday. From this perspective, we may see that it's kind of crazy to spend our lives attaching ourselves (sometimes painfully) to the world around us. The world changes all the time. The things we attach ourselves to will never last. This is yet another reason why it's better to let go of them.

Emperor and Stoic philosopher Marcus Aurelius observed that the nature of the universe is to constantly create and recreate the world.

> *"We find ourselves in a river. Which of the things around us should we value when none of them can offer a firm foothold? Like an attachment to a sparrow: we glimpse it and it's gone. And life itself: like the decoction of blood, the drawing in of air. We expel the power of breathing we drew in at birth (just yesterday or the day before), breathing it out like the air we exhale at each moment."*

Marcus Aurelius, *Meditations*, 6.15

So, we could propose the following lesson in the form of a question: *why hold on tightly to things that are in constant flux?*

3) Residing in the present moment

The third way refers to the human obsession with the past and future. This obsession is understandable. The past probably left a huge impression on us (and may have generated some valuable life lessons), while the future is where we're all headed. The problem, however, is that some people live entirely outside that place where life is happening: the present moment. Their worries about the future make them so uptight and sometimes so paralyzed, while the heavy burden of the past is resting on their shoulders. Marcus Aurelius was aware of the human tendency to live outside the present. I quote:

"The present is the same for everyone; its loss is the same for everyone; and it should be clear that a brief instant is all that is lost. For you can't lose either the past or the future; how could you lose what you don't have?"

Marcus Aurelius, *Meditations*, 2.14

So, 'letting go' in this case means letting go of what we don't have. Sure, we have our thoughts about the past and the future, but what are thoughts but the fabrication of the mind? They don't represent the world around us. They're mere illusions, fantasies, calculations, memories. The mind is a great tool. The Stoics see rational thinking as a gift that sets humans apart from animals and makes it possible for us to live a life of virtue. But *we* must use the tools that we're given and not the other way around because of excessive worry and rumination.

Being Offended

It's quite easy to offend someone or be offended these days. Even my stating this observation can rub someone up the wrong way. In the age of social media, we get bombarded with crude language, opinions we don't like, and stuff that's downright mean. That's probably why we see an increase in language policing and censorship. To some extent, depending on the context, this can be a good thing, for example, to protect minors. But when it's going too far, we can ask ourselves: *aren't we getting too thin-skinned?*

From a Stoic point of view, we're not offended by what we deem offensive, but by our *choice* to be offended. Words of other people cannot hurt us, unless we let them. Seneca the Younger was a statesman, dramatist, and satirist. But I believe that most of us know him as one of the great Stoic philosophers. He was concerned with the nature of insults and being offended. He wrote down his thoughts on this matter in a work named *De Constantia Sapientis*, which is Latin for *On the Firmness of the Wise Man*. In it he criticized his friend Serenus for wishing that people, in general, didn't offend each other. According to Seneca, this is completely unrealistic and not within our control. Instead, we should aim *not* to be offended, which *is* within our control. This brings us to the first piece of Stoic wisdom that can help us build a thicker skin:

1) Not demanding the world to be nice

The world is full of people that are selfish, insolent, arrogant, ignorant, cruel, conniving, and downright mean. This may sound pessimistic, but as far as I've observed, it's the truth. We cannot expect that people will be nice to us all the time – because they aren't. Humans possess the full gamut of emotions, desires, and mind states: from angry, to happy, from compassionate to sadistic. Also, there are as many opinions as there are people, including opinions we don't agree with. Resisting this, is a recipe for disappointment and will lead us to get offended all the time by what's simply a product of nature. Demanding that the world doesn't offend us is futile because it's impossible to alter more than seven billion people to our own liking. As Seneca stated:

> *"You are expressing a wish that the whole human race were inoffensive, which may hardly be; moreover, those who would gain by such wrongs not being done are those who would do them, not he who could not suffer from them even if they were done."*

Lucius Annaeus Seneca, *On The Firmness Of The Wise Man*, 4

Now, even though we cannot demand that everyone always be nice to us, this doesn't mean that we should put up with people who treat us badly. We can set boundaries, and choose not to spend time – or at least limit our interactions – with people that don't respect us. But, if we accept that *people will be people* including their darker side, we'll not only have a much easier time here on earth, we will also give our fellow human beings the right to exist and speak their minds.

2) Accepting the truth, rejecting nonsense

In my first book, *Unoffendable*, I made a proposition inspired by the work of Seneca, on how to handle insults based on truthfulness. With this method, it's logically impossible to be offended. Before I continue, let's take a look at what Seneca had to say about handling insults, jokes, and other stuff that people may throw at us.

> *"Someone has made a joke about the baldness of my head, the weakness of my eyes, the thinness of my legs, the shortness of my stature; what insult is there in telling me that which everyone sees?"*

Lucius Annaeus Seneca, *On The Firmness of the Wise Man*, 16

Now, the approach is very simple. If someone offends you, ask yourself if the thing that you feel offended by is *truth* or *nonsense*. If it's the truth, why be offended by the truth? Or, as Seneca states: "What insult is there in telling me that which everyone sees?" If it's nonsense, why be offended by nonsense? If someone throws nonsense at us, isn't the person that does so the one who should feel ashamed, instead of us?

3) Contemplating ego

Seneca noticed that, for some reason, people think that being insulted is one of the worst things that can happen:

"...many think that there is nothing more bitter than insult; thus you will find slaves who prefer to be flogged to being slapped, and who think stripes and death more endurable than insulting words."

Lucius Annaeus Seneca, *On The Firmness of the Wise Man*, 5

Being slapped was a grave insult in Seneca's time. He was a contemporary of Jesus Christ. So it's no surprise that the Bible speaks about 'showing the other cheek' after being slapped. In this context, 'slapped' doesn't mean physical assault but, rather, an insult. When we are insulted, our ego is attacked. This is a consequence of the story we tell ourselves *about* ourselves and how the world should be. That's why we see that in different cultures and subcultures people are offended by different things. When something conflicts with our narrative

64

(whatever that may be), this could lead to feeling offended.

The questions we could ask ourselves are these: *why* are we getting offended? What's the root of this? Is it because of something that has happened in the past? Is it because of a certain ideology? Is it because I've been culturally conditioned to be offended by this? In my opinion, it shows much more character if we try and seek the root of our emotional reactions within ourselves, instead of immediately finger-pointing at the outside world. Our inner faculty is our responsibility, and what other people think is none of our business.

Anger (feat. Buddhism)

⚬⊰⊱⊙⊰⊱⚬

"Of what use is anger, when the same end can be arrived at by reason? Do you suppose that a hunter is angry with the beasts he kills?"

Lucius Annaeus Seneca, *Of Anger*, 1.11

Anger is an emotion that everyone experiences at some point in their lives. There are different ways in which anger manifests and also different ways to handle it. Some people throw temper tantrums when they don't get their way; others respond with anger when they are in danger, and a respectable number of people cling to the idea of 'being wronged' which results in a form of anger that slowly consumes us. This is also known as 'resentment.' Even though anger is natural, we cannot deny that the consequences of unrelenting and uncontrolled anger can be devastating. It's not uncommon that anger leads to murder. Moreover, history has taught us that deeply rooted anger, also called 'hate,' can lead to mass violence, war, and even genocide.

Still, many people justify anger, calling it 'righteous anger' when they have solid reasons to be angry. Also, people see anger as a functional emotion that assists us in asserting and defending ourselves. Aristotle declared anger to be the desire to repay suffering. We could also see anger as a form of energy, and when harvested skillfully, such energy may help us to attain our goals. Stoic philosopher Seneca, however, is critical of the validity of these claims, telling us that anger is a form of madness:

> *"..for it is equally devoid of self-control, regardless of decorum, forgetful of kinship, obstinately engrossed in whatever it begins to do, deaf to reason and advice, excited by trifling causes, awkward at perceiving what is true and just, and very like a falling rock which breaks itself to pieces upon the very thing which it crushes."*

Lucius Annaeus Seneca, *Of Anger*, 1.1

There is a Buddhist story that challenges the notion of righteous anger. It tells of a young boy with a bad temper. His father was concerned about the angry outbursts of his son. But, instead of fighting anger with anger, he gave the boy a bag of nails and a hammer. He told him to hammer a nail into the fence every time he lost his temper. After the first day, the boy hammered about thirty nails in the fence. But when the days passed, the daily number of nails decreased until the day came that the boy didn't lose his temper once. He proudly told his father, who gave his son the instruction to pull out a nail every time he was able to suppress his temper. Finally, the day arrived that all the nails were pulled out. The father

67

showed his son the fence and said: "Well done, my son! Now, I want you to look closely at the fence. It's full of holes, which means that it has been changed forever. When you let anger out, it will leave scars. You can stick a knife in someone and pull it out, but no matter how often you apologize, the scar will be there forever."

Even when we may seem to have a very good reason to be angry, which is a sense of being wronged and violated, we only risk doing further damage if we throw our ability to reason in the gutter and let our emotions take over. "When reason ends, anger begins," said the Dalai Lama.

Now, there are many different forms of anger. There is rage, surliness, resentment, bitterness, harshness; there is temporary anger that lasts a few minutes, and long-term anger that lasts a lifetime. Tibetan Buddhist monk Geshe YongDong distinguished two types of anger: *hot anger* and *cold anger*. The first type of anger is the one that, figuratively speaking, sets oneself and the surroundings on fire. The second type of anger is the one that's internalized and repressed, and can be carried along for years, eating one up inside.

Seeing our reasoning ability as the fundamental difference between animals and humans, Seneca says that we should not confuse human anger with the aggression we see in animals. Human anger is based on flawed reasoning, while animal aggression is based on impulses. Seneca doubts the usefulness of anger for humanity, by explaining the nature of anger compared to the nature of man:

> *"Yet what is more savage against them than anger? Mankind is born for mutual assistance, anger for mutual ruin: the former loves society, the latter estrangement. The one loves to do good, the other to do harm; the one to help even strangers, the other to attack even its dearest friends. The one is ready even to sacrifice itself for the good of others, the other to plunge into peril provided it drags others with it."*

Lucius Annaeus Seneca, *Of Anger*, 1.5

Now, is anger useful? Both Buddhist and Stoic ideas agree on one point: anger is *not* useful. The Dalai Lama pointed this out in his book *A Policy of Kindness*, stating that anger is not necessary when we have the power of reason. Moreover, when we resort to using force, we probably don't have good reasons to do so:

> *"If there are sound reasons or bases for the points you demand, then there is no need to use violence. On the other hand, when there is no sound reason that concessions should be made to you but mainly your own desire, then reason cannot work and you have to rely on force. Thus,*

*using force is not a sign of strength but rather a
sign of weakness."*

Dalai Lama, *A Policy of Kindness*

Therefore, when we are about to throw a tantrum, it's always good to ask ourselves the following question: am I doing this from a place of power or a place of powerlessness? According to Seneca, there is nothing reason cannot do what anger can. In his work, *Of Anger*, he makes a distinction between 'using force' and 'using force with anger.' In some situations, it is necessary to use force. Many people believe that using force goes together with anger and that being angry can somehow assist them in their use of force. But Seneca compared anger to drunkenness; in a battle, angry fighters have no control over their movements, like drunks. Eventually, their rashness leads to defeat by a more intelligent opponent that isn't led by the passions, and thus, acts with greater mental clarity.

So, what can we do about anger? Anger comes in different stages. It may start with a slight irritation which thereafter builds up to an outburst. When the latter is the case, it's too late. Seneca argues that, to remedy anger, we should become aware of it in the early stages, and apply antidotes when it's still small:

*"That which is diseased can never bear to be
handled without complaining: it is best,*

70

therefore, to apply remedies to oneself as soon as we feel that anything is wrong, to allow oneself as little license as possible in speech, and to restrain one's impetuosity: now it is easy to detect the first growth of our passions: the symptoms precede the disorder."

Lucius Annaeus Seneca, *Of Anger*, 3.12

Thus it's clear that the Stoics prefer tranquility to anger. But how do they achieve this? In Buddhist as well as Stoic sources we'll find different approaches and ideas that can help to kick anger to the curb. An important one is 'patience.' Patience, according to Seneca, is a product of reason. Patience is also conformable to the Buddhist doctrine of 'impermanence.' Everything is in flux and what's happening at this moment will soon be the past. Not only will the things that we are upset about lose their significance, the feelings of anger will start to subside. That's why 'counting to ten' is excellent advice – although, in some cases, it may be better to count to a hundred! Nevertheless, by having patience, we become a companion of time.

When we're already angry, it's helpful to acknowledge that we're angry. This doesn't mean that we have to act it out; it's just that we are aware that this emotion is present in our body and accept this. We suppress it without denying its presence. If we deny the fact that we're angry because, for example, we insist on being goody-goodies that never get angry (regardless of our true feelings), we're fooling ourselves and the world. We can calmly say to someone: "I feel angry right now," without punching that person in the nose. When we acknowledge our anger, we create space between the observer and the emotion, without identification with that emotion. This way, it won't control us.

Another solution is forgiveness, which works better when it comes to long-term (cold) anger. When we forgive, we can finally permit ourselves to let go of the grudges that we've been carrying around for so long. The Stoic idea of 'control' is a good argument to practice forgiveness: some things are in our control, some things just aren't. We can't change the past; we can't control what the person who wronged us says, does, or feels. But we can change our position towards all of this. We can let go and forgive. Or we can choose to drink poison and wait for the other person to perish, even though it's more likely that this leads to our own, slow, and painful death.

Crisis

This piece was written at the beginning of the global COVID-19 pandemic in 2020, and explores how Stoic philosophy can help us cope in times of crisis.

When a crisis is upon us, how can we deal with it the Stoic way? When we look at Stoic literature, we'll find some nuggets of wisdom that we can apply during such times of hardship. Crises come in many different forms. We can have personal crises, but we can also be faced with a global crisis that hits us all. The nature of crises is that we are temporarily in a different state, often characterized by danger and with an acute need for measures and solutions. Being in a crisis doesn't have to affect our behavior in a bad way. In fact, as opposed to what's happening around us, we're still in control of our actions. This doesn't remove the fact that crises can be highly stressful and cause many to suffer.

Marcus Aurelius endured many hardships during his reign as leader of the most powerful empire in the world. He faced not only war, but also the plague that broke out in the East, which eventually caused the death of five million Romans. Among the victims was Lucius Verus, who was not only Marcus Aurelius' adoptive brother but also reigned with him as co-emperor. In his *Meditations*, a theme that Marcus Aurelius frequently writes about is the human connection between each other and nature. In a crisis that affects a lot of people, the awareness of our connectedness is critical, when it comes to coping, supporting each other, and finding solutions. Hence, the first one:

1) Working together, playing your part

As you may know by now, Stoicism isn't about becoming an emotionless rock. It's about *virtue*. And part of virtue is acting for the benefit of the world and humanity. Marcus Aurelius emphasizes that we're interdependent, and therefore, we're not supposed to be egotistical hermits that only think of themselves. That concept is appealing, I know, especially when living in a free and individualistic society in which we can go our separate ways. But when a crisis hits, we're again reminded of how much our lives rely on external factors like technology and other people. The structures we're living in are threatened. And when the system fails us, we will be condemned to living, possibly on a more primitive level. Hence, during times of crisis, it's particularly important to recognize our connection and set our egos aside to help a fellow human, relying on our ability to forgive and tolerate, instead of solely engaging in selfish pursuits.

As Marcus Aurelius wrote in his *Meditations*:

"We were born to work together like feet, hands, and eyes, like the two rows of teeth, upper and lower. To obstruct each other is unnatural. To feel anger at someone, to turn your back on him: these are obstructions."

Marcus Aurelius, *Meditations*, 1.1

2) Doing what you can, accepting what you can't

When we deal with our fellow humans, we'll undoubtedly be confronted with people that are selfish, irrational, overly emotional, mean, violent, greedy, hostile, and intolerant. Some people are in full panic mode and go overboard when it comes to taking measures to protect themselves. With their heightened survival instincts, their main focus is self-preservation. There's nothing wrong with 'self-preservation,' of course, but when it becomes an obsession, it may damage those around us and only worsen the situation. And then we have those people who see a crisis as an opportunity to con people and make some big bucks out of it.

When the behavior of others irritates us, it's essential to remember that we only control our own actions. We cannot control how people behave and whether or not they will violate the measures necessary to improve the situation. We cannot control various aspects of the crisis itself, and how everything plays out. Therefore, we rely on our thinking capacity to navigate ourselves through the crisis, regardless of how it unfolds. It's up to *us* how we act. And to act despite the actions of others is all we can do.

3) Adapting to a new situation

A crisis goes together with change. When we're stuck in our routines for so long and have taken our lifestyles and the comforts of society for granted, a crisis can be a very humbling as well as frightening experience. Things that seemed so normal and stable have suddenly become uncertain. The economy takes a hit, with all the consequences. Necessary measures to fight the crisis lead to the disruption of our daily affairs. It shows us that we, despite our technological advancements, are still very vulnerable and that our wellbeing isn't automatically assured. Especially in times of turmoil, we're forced to weigh in on our ability to adapt. To do this, it's essential to accept the changing nature of the universe, so we can let go of the past and things we took for granted. We can focus on the present and make the best out of it.

"Change and flux constantly remake the world, just as the incessant progression of time remakes eternity. We find ourselves in a river. Which of the things around us should we value when none of them can offer a firm foothold? Like an

attachment to a sparrow: we glimpse it and it's
gone."

Marcus Aurelius, *Meditations*, 6.15

Worry

This piece was written at the beginning of the global COVID-19 pandemic in 2020, and explores how Stoic philosophy can help us cope in times of crisis.

"Worse than war is the very fear of war."

Lucius Annaeus Seneca, *Tragedies*, Thyestes, line 572 (Chorus)

Human history has never been free from adversity. Events like war, the outbreak of plagues and natural disasters have caused dark times tainted by suffering and death. Without a doubt, the ancient Stoics had their fair share of hardship and the difficulties of life are the core of their philosophical writings. In hard times of great uncertainty, many people start worrying about their stable comfortable lives falling apart. The prospect of undergoing significant change at the hands of misfortune, not knowing where these changes lead to, can even be more nerve-racking. The Stoics had some profound things to say about dealing with external circumstances, and how to live peacefully in the face of hardship and a troubled future.

Living in a society in which mass consumption is the norm, and companies brainwash us into believing that we *need* their products to feel complete, the distinction between what we truly need and what's obsolete has become blurred. In wealthy countries, people rarely concern themselves with their basic needs, because these

78

are a given. But when hard times are knocking on our doors, it's time to create clarity. We will now have to decide what our priorities are, and learn to deal with uncertainty.

First of all, it's essential to remember the 'dichotomy of control' and to be constantly aware of the fact that we only control our own actions. According to Epictetus, things like our body, property, and reputation are not up to us. When the economy declines, for example, there isn't much we can do about it. We could lose a lot of money in the stock market as well as our jobs, and, thus, our income. But from a Stoic point of view, by tying our happiness to these things in the first place, we have already set ourselves up for disappointment. It's never a bad thing to remind ourselves of the famous words by Epictetus:

> *"The things in our control are by nature free, unrestrained, unhindered; but those not in our control are weak, slavish, restrained, belonging to others. Remember, then, that if you suppose that things which are slavish by nature are also free, and that what belongs to others is your own, then you will be hindered."*

Epictetus, *Enchiridion*, 1

As mentioned earlier in this book, the Stoics make a distinction between virtue, vice, and indifferents (see chapter 'Happiness'). Virtue and vice correspond with our actions. For example, doing something for the benefit of the community, especially in difficult times, like providing food to the poor and elderly, can be considered virtuous. Trying to sell essential goods at exorbitant prices during a crisis can be considered a vice. But indifferents are neither good nor bad and they are beyond our control. Now, why is this important? What characterizes difficult times is that these indifferents are threatened, but *not* our ability to act. Does that mean that we shouldn't care about these external things at all? Not necessarily, as we need at least the basics to survive.

However, when we are facing hard times, we might want to remind ourselves of what these basics are, so we can let go of the rest and stop worrying about them. If we are on the verge of economic collapse, how important is it really to possess all kinds of luxury goods? And during a pandemic, to what extent does 'social status' bring food to the table and protect us from an illness that doesn't discriminate between rich and poor? The more we are attached to these externals, the more we are disturbed by the prospect of losing them. The truth is, one can be perfectly happy and content without them.

Another essential Stoic lesson concerns death and suffering. This may sound blunt, but, at the end of the day, death and suffering are part of nature. In the West, mentioning this is kind of taboo. Death is seen as something negative, something tragic, and something to be avoided at all costs. And our comfortable lives minimize the amount of pain and suffering as much as possible. But in hard times, we may want to consider that no one is entitled to a long and healthy life. The history of our planet is bloody. Animals and humans kill each other every day, children die at birth, people die from cancer, heart disease, diabetes, strokes, AIDS, traffic incidents…the list goes on. Even though humanity is getting better and better at minimizing such things, we're still ultimately at the mercy of the ways of nature.

Memento mori means the remembrance of death (see chapter 'Memento Mori'). By reminding ourselves that suffering and death are an inescapable and inherent part of life, we might find some tranquility in the idea that we're simply experiencing the inevitable and natural. Seneca, who died peacefully like Socrates, saw relief in death.

> *"Death is a release from and an end of all pains: beyond it, our sufferings cannot extend: it restores us to the peaceful rest in which we lay before we were born. If anyone pities the dead, he ought also to pity those who have not been born."*

Lucius Annaeus Seneca, *Of Consolation: To Marcia*, 19

A final piece of Stoic advice for finding a sense of calm in adversity is to remind ourselves that our destiny isn't up to us. We can influence the future by our actions in the present, but the results are so dependent on external circumstances that it's impossible to guarantee a certain outcome. The economy may fall apart, we may lose our jobs, mass poverty may kick in, and huge numbers of people may pass away: no single 'worry' can change that. So why don't we allow ourselves to just let go of the burden of the future, knowing that, whatever happens, we are in full control of the most powerful weapon available: our inner faculty.

If we can cope with death, we can also cope with life. The good news is that everything is in flux, and born out of change, like night and day, fall and spring. All this, too, shall pass. History has shown us that people have endured the hardest of times and that this experience has often made them more humble, more humane, and more grateful for life. Thus, every outcome has its positive side. And, regardless of what the future brings, no one takes away our power to make the best of it.

Panic

⊸❥❧☙❦⊷

This piece was written at the beginning of the global COVID-19 pandemic in 2020, and explores how Stoic philosophy can help us cope in times of crisis.

How should we act when people around us are panicking? And how can we avoid panicking ourselves? Panic gets us nowhere as it's a state of emotional turmoil during which we throw our rationality overboard. So, when we're faced with a wide variety of opinions, the strong language of influencers, and decisions based on fear and greed, it can be difficult enough to find direction and maintain the course. But, during times of mass hysteria, it's essential to use our capacity for rationality. From a Stoic point of view, our decisions should be based on facts and reason, and our actions have to be in the interest of the common good. In times of hardship, it's not an unnecessary exercise to fortify our minds with philosophical ideas so that we don't slip into the trap of panic. Marcus Aurelius had some valuable insights on how to strengthen the mind, so we don't deviate from the right path.

1) When we're panicking ourselves

To navigate our minds back towards tranquility, it's important to become aware of the *nature* of what we are panicking about, and also the reasons why we panic. In his *Meditations*, Marcus Aurelius mentions that, no matter what happens, it's something that has happened before. When we are ruled by the issues of the day, we lose sight of the bigger picture. Hence, what unfolds at this moment may seem new and alien. In a way, this is true, because nothing that happens now takes place in the past. However, when we look at historical accounts, we see that they are filled with the same old, same old. Marcus Aurelius shifts the paradigm by pointing out that life is simply history repeating itself. So, we could say that we experience the same archetypal storylines over and over again, just with different characters and in different formats. Lost all your money? Your job? Millions of people are going through the same thing as we speak, and have been in the past. Is the world ravaged by the plague? We had the Spanish Flu, the Black Death, SARS, MERS, and more recently, the COVID-19 outbreak. Humanity has gone through many different crises, individual people have faced a lot of hardship in their lives, there have been good times and bad times, and we have gone through war and peace. History has taught us that this mechanism never changes as long as we exist. It's simply life manifesting the same patterns. Everything is transient, like yin and yang.

But why do we panic when it's just another manifestation of the same? Probably because what we panic about has disguised itself as something unprecedented and triggers the fear of the unknown, while, in reality, it has happened many times before. What's new and scary now will be old and familiar tomorrow. That's because we are adaptable creatures who can change along with the transient nature of the universe. To keep a cool head when things around us start to change quickly, we might want to repeat the following quote by Marcus Aurelius:

"No matter what happens, keep this in mind: It's the same old thing, from one end of the world to the other. It fills the history books, ancient and modern, and the cities, and the houses too. Nothing new at all. Familiar, transient."

Marcus Aurelius, *Meditations*, 7.1

All this comes down to seeing things as they are, as much as possible, and doing the right thing based on rationality instead of fear. Thus, in a crisis, we ought to prepare for contingency but not overdo it, especially when it undermines the community. Marcus Aurelius emphasizes repeatedly that we should work together. Or, as he puts it: *"to do what the community needs done."* He argued that what benefits the whole is good for every part of the whole. When we panic, we are often inclined to act unintelligently and in ways that only make things worse, or overlook the things that need to be done. That's why it's essential to keep calm in the face of adversity and assess what's best for ourselves and the community so that we don't mess things up even more. Also, we may want to keep in mind that the media are companies motivated by profit, so they recreate and inflate reality by constantly focusing on sensational topics that attract attention. When we expose ourselves to the media all day, we become deluded because we start to believe that there's nothing else going on in the world besides disaster. This is simply not true.

2) When those around us are panicking

When it comes to dealing with panicking people, staying calm in the herd is much easier when our inner faculties are strong. If we are determined and don't let ourselves be carried away by our irrational thoughts and emotions, we become towers of strength that are immune to all compulsion – like, for example, the tussle in the supermarket for toilet paper that we saw at the beginning of the COVID-19 outbreak. Even when world leaders act irrationally and the things they say don't make any sense, or when hostility and violence run rampant in the streets and people scream blue murder, Marcus Aurelius would probably advise us to not engage with all of that and to calmly do what the situation asks of us.

"Let them scream whatever they want. Let animals dismember this soft flesh that covers you. How would any of that stop you from keeping your mind calm—reliably sizing up what's around you—and ready to make good use of whatever happens?"

Marcus Aurelius, *Meditations*, 7.68

And at the end of the day, what the people around us do is not up to us. If they feel that panic is the answer, we can only change their minds if they're open to alternatives. But when they aren't, we'll only waste time trying. In such cases, we are better off restraining *ourselves* from going along with their panic, so we maintain our inner peace.

Financial Stress

——————— ⚬⤳⧁⧀⤳⚬ ———————

According to the results of a survey by the American Psychological Association, money concerns top the list of the most frequently cited sources of stress. It's no surprise that money problems affect people so much, as these are a direct threat to one's self-preservation. Financial problems can impact us in many different degrees of severity.

Sometimes money problems result in people losing their homes or not having the opportunity of possessing one. Some people are so poor that it's a daily struggle to obtain food – but they are happy nonetheless. Other people have to sell their second holiday home in southern France because of a financial setback, and experience dread. So, the way we perceive a situation plays a role in how much stress we experience. Nevertheless, when we experience financial stress for whatever reason, the Stoics have some good advice for us.

1) Getting back to the basics

Being closely related to the school of the Cynics, the ancient Stoics didn't put too much value on material wealth. For them, *time* is the greatest commodity. Also, they saw our ability to choose and act as much more valuable than any amount of money we would ever have.

Wealth is nice, for sure. But it isn't a necessary ingredient for happiness. We need food and shelter to survive. And, for the majority of the world's population (even in the poorer regions of the world), this bare minimum is available. If you've been able to buy this book, then your basic needs are most likely met. However, it's only human not to be satisfied with the little (or much) we have. On top of our basic needs, we want more. We don't want food; we want expensive tasty food. We don't want clothing; we want designer clothing. We don't want just a roof over our heads; we want a large house with many bedrooms and a garden with a swimming pool.

So, to satisfy our ever-increasing desires, we need money. Lots of it. And if we're able to achieve a certain living standard, we become attached to it. Hence, when the money tap suddenly goes from wide open to almost turned off, we become very restless, even when we still have plenty of financial resources to take care of the necessities. So, why can't we do (at least temporarily) with less? Is it because we want to keep up with the Jones's? Do we have a social circle that emphasizes status? Or perhaps we are afraid that our loved ones will leave us when the money dries up? By the way: using money to attract love isn't a reliable strategy according to Seneca, as he stated: "Fidelity purchased with money, money can destroy." Moreover, wealth can be a great source of misery if we attach great importance to it. Not only will we fear being poor; we'll also *feel* poor when we meet someone wealthier than ourselves.

> *"Suppose that you hold wealth to be a good: poverty will then distress you, and, which is most pitiable, it will be an imaginary poverty. For you may be rich, and nevertheless, because your neighbour is richer, you suppose yourself to be poor exactly by the same amount in which you fall short of your neighbour."*

Lucius Annaeus Seneca, *Moral letters to Lucilius*, 104.9

As far as the Stoics are concerned, anything that goes beyond survival is extraneous and is no requirement for happiness. It's nice to have social status, for example, but we must be willing to give that up if that's the price to pay for tranquility.

2) Focusing on what we can influence

There's no single worry in the world that can stop bad things from happening. Yet, when we struggle financially, we're often immersed in the future and try to control things that we have no power over. Although we may greatly fear losing our money and not being able to pay the bills, having money doesn't take away the strongest tool we have, which is our ability to act. Thinking about the future impedes us from taking action, and the more we worry, the more depleted we feel and the less energy we have to make a change. At some point, we must shift our focus from our fantasies of doom and gloom to the only workspace we have: the present. The present is where the future is made. Only what we can change, *right now*, is what counts. So, instead of staring at a long, endless road of obstacles, we're better off compartmentalizing what needs to be done and then focusing on the task at hand.

3) Asking for help

When we look at the way people behave during a crisis (like the COVID-19 crisis, for example) one could conclude that we're naturally inclined to help a fellow human. Helping people feels good, which probably explains this inclination. The Stoics observed that everything nature comes up with has a part in the play. We're all in this together. By helping each other out in difficult times, we act for the benefit of the whole. Everything is interconnected and we depend on our surroundings. We depend on the oxygen we breathe, on the powerplant that supplies our homes with electricity, on the people that pick up our trash, and so forth. "No man is an island," the English poet John Donne famously wrote. So, isn't refusing to ask for help in an interdependent world kind of insane? In his *Meditations*,

Marcus Aurelius wrote that we shouldn't be afraid to lean on each other, if necessary.

> *"Don't be ashamed to need help. Like a soldier storming a wall, you have a mission to accomplish. And if you've been wounded and you need a comrade to pull you up? So what?"*

Marcus Aurelius, *Meditations*, 7.7

4) Remembering that you're not alone

Many wealthy people live in a bubble. They, with their little social circle of other wealthy people, live in a posh neighborhood, and concern themselves with things that occupy rich people. But, in comparison with the rest of the world, they're a small minority. The vast majority of human beings aren't rich (many of them can be considered poor, or live from paycheck to paycheck). But they still live decent lives. From that perspective, it's hard to imagine that one can be miserable because of not being able to buy a sailboat. But this happens.

Seneca was aware of the burden that the rich bear, which can be summarized as follows: *what you have, you can lose.* Having a certain living standard means that we can lose it. Having money means that we can lose it. Gaining respect from our environment (because we're able to afford a sailboat) means that we can lose it. Hence, the wealthy, once they've obtained their riches, are often terrified of losing them. But is this truly a fate to be fearful about? Well, it depends. If we descend into poverty, we lose access to luxury and may lose our rich 'friends' as well, meaning that if we're attached to these externals, we'll suffer. But if one door closes, many others open. We may be cast out of our wealthy bubble, but we'll be accompanied by the majority of our kind. As Seneca stated: "I may become a poor man; I shall then be one among many."

5) Putting your tranquility first

The teachings of Epictetus are very clear about this: our peace of mind is more important than outside affairs. This doesn't mean that we shouldn't try to improve our financial situation if we can, but from a Stoic perspective, we must set our priorities straight. Looking for work, doubling down on our businesses, finding ways to make money on the side are ways to get us out of a financially unfavorable situation. But should we sacrifice our mental wellbeing for it? This is what Epictetus said about it:

> *"If you want to improve, reject such reasonings as these: "If I neglect my affairs, I'll have no income; if I don't correct my servant, he will be bad." For it is better to die with hunger, exempt from grief and fear, than to live in affluence with*

*perturbation; and it is better your servant should
be bad, than you unhappy."*

Epictetus, *Enchiridion*, 12

Epictetus' attitude may seem unrealistic and extreme, but it's food for thought if we're in a situation of despair. The Stoics value time more than anything. Regardless of how bad the circumstances are, they'd argue that we must always aim for happiness and inner peace. Paradoxically, by setting our worries aside and prioritizing tranquility, we'll often experience that we're better able to handle the situation when we come from a place of inner peace. A simple method that may bring some relief in the face of an uncertain future is *amor fati* (see chapters 'Love of fate' and 'Amor fati').

6) Remembering what you *do* have

Lastly, we tend to overlook the things we already have because we focus on the things we lack. This is probably the case because we take so many things for granted and forget how blessed we are. Marcus Aurelius teaches us to ignore what we don't have, and try to imagine what it's like to not have what we have.

*"Look at what you have, the things you value
most, and think of how much you'd crave them if
you didn't have them. But be careful. Don't feel*

such satisfaction that you start to overvalue them,
that it would upset you to lose them."

Marcus Aurelius, *Meditations*, 7.27

Marcus Aurelius warns us, however, to not become overly attached to things to the point that we'd be 'upset' if we lost them. So, approaching possessions the Stoic way is a delicate process. On the one hand, we are to be content with what we have (and not desire what we haven't). On the other, we are to be detached enough from what we have so losing it won't disturb us.

Loneliness

For many people, the feeling of dissatisfaction that comes with being alone is a heavy cross to bear. There's hardly consensus about how much human connection we truly need. Some scientists suggest that we need company as much as food, while others would argue that humans can be alone for long periods without any difficulty. Humanity has known many hermits who purposefully chose the solitary existence and didn't die from being alone as one would starve from not eating.

Stoicism as a philosophy emphasizes working together, helping our fellow humans, and being of service. However, according to Epictetus, we must keep in mind that sometimes we cannot escape the situation of being alone. Being alone (or in solitude) isn't necessarily wrong. What counts is what we make of it. Interestingly enough, Epictetus makes a distinction between 'forlornness' (also called eremia) and being 'alone' (monaxia). The state of 'forlornness' he compares to being helpless, as we would if we encountered a bunch of robbers when traveling alone. There's also an element of forsakenness and 'being lost' in the concept of eremia. Epictetus is clear that, when one is alone, one isn't necessarily forlorn. Otherwise, he argues, Zeus himself would be forlorn as he's up there alone in the sky. But Zeus as the chief of the gods is anything but forlorn.

According to Epictetus, those who indeed believe that Zeus is unhappy in his solitude, cannot comprehend the mode of life of a solitary being, as they're inclined by nature to be gregarious.

Human beings are social creatures, and we indeed tend to look for each other. Being part of a group has many benefits. We feel protected, as we're stronger together than by ourselves. We feel connected, as we have people to communicate with. Also, in many cases, social interaction makes life fun and interesting. But spending time alone is also part of life, a part that many people fear or try to shut out. Many people had rather be in destructive relationships than alone. Epictetus states that spending time alone is also part of life and that we shouldn't shut the door to this experience:

> *"But nevertheless a man must prepare himself for solitude too—he must be able to suffice for himself, and able to commune with himself. Just as Zeus communes with Himself and is at peace with Himself and reflects upon the nature of His government, and occupies Himself with thoughts appropriate to Himself, so should we be able to talk to ourselves, without need of others, or craving for diversion."*

Epictetus, *Discourses*, 3.13

We're not in control of our circumstances. No matter how great our social skills are, and how many friends we've accumulated over the years; Fortune doesn't guarantee that we'll never be alone. External factors are fickle, and so are social connections. One day we may be surrounded by friends that provide us with the joy of companionship; another, we may be abandoned. Moreover, we're born alone and die alone. Aloneness is as much part of life as companionship. And when we don't know how to be in our own company, we'll surely be confronted with feelings of loneliness. Moreover, when we look at the world, the interconnectedness between ourselves and nature, and how we are part of one big ecosystem, sharing land and sea with so many other beings, feeling lonely doesn't make much sense.

Epictetus tells us that even children know how to entertain themselves when they're left alone: "They pick up potsherds and dust and build something or other and then pull it down and build something else again, and so they never lack diversion." He urges us not to be worse than children and, when we find ourselves alone, we should also take our potsherds and dust and build something. Without a doubt, Epictetus' words are spoken metaphorically and could be explained like this: to not feel forlorn, we must develop the skills to entertain ourselves and to be occupied with ourselves when we're alone. Instead of shedding tears because someone has left us, or weep because we're without company, having ourselves to fall back on is paramount.

In my own experience, learning to enjoy solitude can be done by deliberately choosing solitude. And when solitude isn't our own choice, we can convert it to an opportunity to become more *self-sufficient*. In today's world, in particular, there are countless ways to entertain ourselves. The internet has become an almost inexhaustible resource of information. Then, we have access to thousands (if not more) of movies, books, television series, and video games. We can write, paint, draw, make something beautiful out of clay. We can meditate, do physical exercise, do breathing exercises. The possibilities are endless and go far beyond the entertainment value of potsherds and dust.

As Jean-Paul Sartre once stated: "If you are lonely when you are alone, you are in bad company." When we're happy by ourselves we don't need other people to keep us company. This way, we increase our independence of outside circumstances. Socializing, then, becomes optional rather than necessary. And even though we might prefer company over solitude, nonetheless, the ability to be content with the circumstances of a particular stage in life relieves us of the pain of loneliness.

Guilt

We experience guilt when we believe that we've done something wrong. This wrongdoing could have been intentional or accidental. The degree of guilt one experiences seems to vary from person to person. Some people feel guilty after committing the smallest of errors; other people commit terrible crimes and don't experience any guilt. Nevertheless, guilt can be functional. It's an emotion that tells us that there's something wrong. From guilt may arise an effort to restore one's faults, to offer an apology, and to do things differently in the future. Repentance of one's sins can be seen as a good thing if it leads to an overall decrease in human suffering. Thus, guilt mostly involves a sense of justice as well as compassion when we're confronted with other people's suffering as a consequence of our actions. But in many cases, one's experience of guilt goes beyond what's functional to become destructive.

1) The destructiveness of guilt

When one is guilt-ridden there's a tendency of ongoing self-disapproval. We can suffer day-in and day-out by a memory of something we did in the past. Whether or not this is good or bad is in the eye of the beholder. According to some, we must suffer extensively when we've done something wrong. Even though suffering is imposed on us already in the form of punishment, they expect us to feel bad about ourselves for a long time on top of that. This is seen as justice served and revenge on behalf of the victim(s). But in the long run, ongoing guilt doesn't serve any purpose except in fulfilling the wishes of those that want to see us suffer. Some people even use someone's guilt as a control mechanism to make this person feel indebted and, therefore, obligated to make reparation for their badness.

There's even a worse type of guilt that comes with the idea of being inherently bad –
just for being alive. This idea can be enforced by parents, abusive partners, or toxic environments in which people have contempt for us because, for example, of the way we look. In such cases, we can speak of 'toxic guilt.' Toxic guilt is a paralyzing emotion and it's often associated with depression, feelings of worthlessness, social isolation and avoidance, anxiety, and even suicide. By reading the ancient Stoic scriptures, I've discovered a few guidelines that we can use to handle 'guilt.'

2) Repentance and punishment

When we're feeling guilty, the first thing we need is clarity which we can obtain by mindfully assessing the situation. Why are we feeling guilty? What have we done? To what degree are we to blame? Justice is one of the cardinal virtues in Stoicism and requires us to be honest and fair. If we're truly at fault, then we'd better admit to that, accept the consequences and correct our mistakes, if possible. In one of his letters to Lucilius, Seneca writes the following:

> *"Why will no man confess his faults? Because he is still in their grasp; only he who is awake can recount his dream, and similarly a confession of sin is a proof of sound mind. Let us, therefore, rouse ourselves, that we may be able to correct our mistakes."*

Lucius Annaeus Seneca, *Moral Letters to Lucilius*, 53.8

However, Seneca doesn't believe in punishment (even though punishment is part of today's judicial system) as he sees "the punishment of crime lies in the crime itself." The consequences of bad deeds, he argues, are much worse than the penalties we tend to impose on offenders. Just think about the drug dealer that sleeps with a gun on his nightstand in constant fear of his life. Or think about how people naturally avoid wrongdoers for their own safety, and the loneliness this brings. Seneca argues that we can escape our penalty due to sheer luck, but we cannot escape our conscience and will suffer internally nonetheless. The feeling of guilt is part of this suffering. "It's the property of guilt to be in fear," Seneca wrote. We'll generate more and more reasons to feel guilty if we don't change our ways. Only if we establish a sound mind can we become aware of our wrongdoings; repent and correct our mistakes, so guilt can subside.

3) The power of change

When we're truly at fault, there's a time for repentance, a time for offering apologies, and even a time for punishment. But, at some point, there's no benefit in feeling guilty except to please those that want to see our suffering continue. Even though their inability to let go of the past is an understandable human flaw, these people don't help themselves either, by wishing for someone else's suffering to ease their pain. This method doesn't work. The sweetness of revenge doesn't last long. It arises from pain and causes pain. It would be better for them to let their grievances go and focus on living their lives happily. Unfortunately, we've got nothing to say about the behavior of other people. Some people take their grudges into their graves after they've inflicted the world around them for years because of their unwillingness to give them up. In the long run, the grudges of other people shouldn't be our problem anymore.

In his *Meditations*, Marcus Aurelius reiterated over and over again the importance of living in the present and letting the past go. He explained that existence flows past us like a river and that we're in constant flux. Things change; people change. The person who's done something awful in the past isn't the same in the present. And what's happened in the past cannot be altered. So, why not *use* change? The past may be over but it's still an invaluable source of life lessons. We cannot apply the things we've learned in that past and undo what we've done, but we *can* apply them in the present. All humans make mistakes. Instead of repeating our faults over and over again, it's much wiser to focus on our lives right now, and show, primarily to ourselves, that we're making a change. A forgiving person understands this and will probably celebrate our efforts to be better. Unforgiving people, however, have always been around and will probably not cease to exist anytime soon.

Stoic Philosophers on Inner Peace

Marcus Aurelius

As emperor of Rome, Marcus Aurelius was the most powerful man on the planet. Yet, as opposed to many of his predecessors and successors, he aimed to live a virtuous life consistently. This lies in sharp contrast with the self-indulgent, hedonistic lifestyles of some of the Roman Emperors. Needless to say, Marcus Aurelius was a busy man, carrying the burden of leadership over an *empire*, with all the stress that comes from this. His work, *Meditations*, gives us an idea of how he coped. To modern Stoics, he is famous for laying the groundwork for the *praemeditatio malorum* (the premeditation of troubles and wickedness that may lie ahead) which they apply as a meditative practice for starting the day. Later in this book, I'll go in-depth into this practice.

In this chapter, I'd like to focus on Marcus Aurelius' lesser-known practical teachings that can aid us in achieving inner peace.

1) Doing less

This is a *no-brainer*, right? To become calmer, we should simply *do less*. Now, it's important to mention that the Stoics hold productivity in high regard, as they see being industrious as a virtue. On the other hand, moderation is a virtue as well. So, how, exactly should we do less, when we're supposed to be industrious? Marcus Aurelius observed that people do many unnecessary things. In the current age, we have access to almost unlimited entertainment, so it's very easy to get caught up in all kinds of non-productive activities. With 'doing less,' Marcus Aurelius also meant 'talking less.' Many conversations are nonsensical, lead to nowhere, and only waste our time and energy. So, 'doing less' actually means 'doing no more than the essential.' And doing no more than the essential not only amounts to cutting out the nonsense, but also working intelligently and efficiently. An advantage that we gain from this (besides tranquility) is that we can do less, better. Doing the essential consistently takes a mindful approach:

> *"If you can eliminate it, you'll have more time, and more tranquility. Ask yourself at every moment, "Is this necessary?" But we need to eliminate unnecessary assumptions as well, to eliminate the unnecessary actions that follow."*

Marcus Aurelius, *Meditations*, 4-24

As mentioned earlier, a great habit that helps us stay focused on our daily endeavors is making a list of tasks the night before. This way, we premeditate on what we have to do when we get up in the morning, which has a calming effect on the mind. When we design our days beforehand, there's less for the mind to worry about.

2) Short escapes

In one of my YouTube-videos, I explained that the Stoics aren't too fond of traveling for recreational purposes, and don't see it as a good way to seek tranquility. The reason is that, wherever we go, we take ourselves with us. This means that the effects of traveling are only temporary. Thus, as soon as the novelty subsides, we'll be confronted with our minds again. Marcus Aurelius was critical of people seeking refuge from their daily worries by traveling or residing in quiet places like the mountains or beaches. In his mind, this was an idiotic thing to do, because why should we travel when we can get away by going within? "Nowhere you can go is more peaceful – freer of interruptions – than your own soul," he said. He nevertheless argued that there's nothing wrong with changing scenery once in a while to facilitate our mental retreats, as long as we keep these escapes basic and brief.

What Marcus Aurelius proposed reminds me a lot of meditation, or perhaps, moments of reflection and contemplation, to renew ourselves so we can calmly carry on with our daily lives. He gave us two things to ponder over if we choose to briefly retreat in our minds.

"That things have no hold on the soul. They stand there unmoving, outside it. Disturbance comes only from within—from our own perceptions."

And:

"That everything you see will soon alter and cease to exist. Think of how many changes you've already seen. The world is nothing but change. Our life is only perception."

Marcus Aurelius, *Meditations*, 4.3

3)   Remembering that all shall pass

The Stoics are infamous for remembering the frightening reality of life: that it's going to end. Remembering death, therefore, is the ultimate acceptance that the changing nature of the universe also means the decay and vanishing of ourselves. Marcus Aurelius tells us to keep in mind how fast things pass us by; one moment we could be immersed in something, and the next moment it could change. Trends come and go in the blink of an eye, and when we look at the history of this planet, human life is just a tiny little hiccup in this cosmic evolution, and will eventually disappear along with everything that it's preoccupied with. As Marcus Aurelius wrote:

"The infinity of past and future gapes before us –
a chasm whose depths we cannot see. So it would
take an idiot to feel self-importance or distress.
Or any indignation, either. As if the things that
irritate us lasted."

Marcus Aurelius, *Meditations*, 5.23

The fact that everything is in flux could be a source of anxiety, because nothing is stable, and eventually we will be separated from our possessions and loved ones. But it can be a source of calm as well. The realization that everything is temporary means that there's no point in clinging to good times and being strongly averse to bad times. Happiness is a relative thing. Even in prison, there are good and bad days. And even millionaires experience joy as well as suffering. This means that no matter what fortune or misfortune befalls us, we'll get used to it anyway. The degree of happiness and sorrow we experience remains dependent on our inner faculties and not on the circumstances. Knowing this, why should we be so concerned about destiny? If anything, it's our inner world, our way of thinking, our perceptions, and judgments that should concern us.

Epictetus

Even though they espoused the same philosophy, Marcus Aurelius was an emperor and Epictetus was a slave. The fact that someone from the lowest class became one of the greatest Stoic philosophers indicates that Stoicism isn't just for the elite: it's for everyone. The works of Epictetus reveal the importance of tranquility, and that we should value this over lesser things like money, reputation, and even the physical body. He tells us that a calm mind is not achieved by trying to alter and control our surroundings: it's achieved by the way we think.

The main work of Epictetus is called *Discourses*, a collection of lectures that a pupil named Arrian wrote down. This same pupil also compiled the *Enchiridion*, which means 'Handbook' and is quite easy to read and digest. From Epictetus' writings, I've distilled the following life lessons that can help us to cope with daily worries, stressful events, and hardships, so we can keep a calm mind regardless of what the world throws at us.

1) Acting in accordance with nature

When Epictetus was teaching, one of his students told him that he wanted to go home, because he was sick. Epictetus then sent him home. But he also asked his student whether or not he thought that with his condition he could improve his moral purpose and, thus, him coming to class was the right thing to do. He said:

"Go back and tend to your affairs at home. For if your governing principle cannot be brought into conformity with nature, no doubt your paltry piece of land can be made to conform with it."

Epictetus, *Discourses*, 3.41

The lesson we take from this is that it's wise to do what the current situation asks of us. Whatever overcomes us is the way of the universe. There's no need to force the issue. So when we're sick, we shouldn't force ourselves to do things we cannot do. In many cases, the best way to treat an illness is accepting it and doing what's best in that given moment. It's true that Epictetus also stated that illness is a hindrance to the body, but not to our ability to choose. This doesn't mean that we should force ourselves to perform our duties, which might only make things worse; it means that despite the physical hindrance, we still can *choose* to (in this case) lose ourselves in panic or make rational choices in a more tranquil fashion. When we look at the outbreak of the COVID-19 pandemic in 2020, for example, we saw two extremes: at one end, there was panic, at the other, complete nonchalance. In the first case, people are overtaken by fear and emotion, and in the second case, people refuse to see the problem and, perhaps, try to appear tough. But acting in accordance

112

with nature, meaning the nature of the universe as well as our human nature, starts by acknowledging the situation, doing the proper research, and taking the necessary measures that fit the circumstances while keeping a cool head. No matter how we choose to react, it's important to remember that sickness and death are simply part of nature. We all go some day. This brings us to the next one:

2) Watching our judgments

Anxiety isn't caused by the environment. It's caused by the position we take *towards* the environment. We all have our frames of reference, and from that frame, we decide what we can tolerate and what we can't. There's nothing wrong with that. Oftentimes, it serves a purpose to discern right from wrong. However, our judgments become a problem if they make us feel entitled to things that we're naturally not entitled to, which is a form of delusion. For example, we can be angry for a lifetime because we feel entitled to the good parents we never had. But Epictetus points out that we are not entitled to a 'good' parent – just to a parent. And this is true for many things. So, why should we feel distressed by entirely natural things?

"Distinguish within your own mind, and be prepared to say, 'It's not the accident that distresses this person, because it doesn't distress

113

another person; it is the judgment which he
makes about it.'"

Epictetus, *Enchiridion*, 16

Again, this is important when we face illness or death. These things are nothing new. They're part of nature as much as war and violence and should rather be approached with equanimity than strong aversion. Moreover, when we don't carry strong desires and aversions (and the strong emotional reactions that may come from that), we're more capable of dealing with the situation in a rational way.

3) Focusing less on things outside of your control

At the beginning of the *Enchiridion*, we'll find the Stoics famous 'dichotomy of control,' which is a cornerstone of Stoic thinking. It emphasizes that some things are up to us, and others are not, so we ought to focus on the former, and have contempt for the latter. As living creatures in this universe, we have to deal with what's around us. We might desire to control the outside world, perhaps by money, a position of power, physical strength, intelligence, or intimidation. But, at the end of the day, these are just instruments of influence but never of (complete) control. And, even if we do manage to control *some* things, there's always a billion other things that slip out of our hands.

There's one thing that we do indeed control, according to Epictetus, which is the inner faculty. And that's what we should focus on. What happens around us isn't that important. It's more important what we do with it. Therefore, we can choose to focus our attention on our thoughts and emotions, rather than constantly worrying about stuff we can't do much about anyway. This doesn't mean that we close ourselves off completely. It means that we develop a healthy indifference towards outside events so that they won't stress us out too much. This is where *amor fati* comes in (see more in the chapters 'Love of fate' and 'Amor fati'). The Stoics ask if there is a better way to deal with the unavoidable than to embrace it.

Seneca

Seneca the Younger was a philosopher who held an important position in the Roman Empire and is one of the major contributors to Stoic philosophy. Seneca's words are as much geared towards indifference, as what we *should* care about to achieve tranquility. Seneca exchanged many letters with his friend Serenus on how to free the mind of anxiety and worry in a Stoic way. One day, Serenus wrote a letter to his friend Seneca, explaining the mental disturbances which were afflicting him in his day-to-day activities and asked Seneca to relieve him of his trouble. Seneca wrote back a letter containing his advice. This dialogue is now called *De Tranquillitate Animi* which is Latin for *"On the Tranquility of the Mind."* So, what did Seneca prescribe for Serenus for becoming a bit more serene? I've distilled seven suggestions from this advice for achieving tranquility.

1) Not relying on hope

Seneca observed that many people are preoccupied with the future and, therefore, hardly have their minds in the present moment. They are filled with their long-range desires and geared towards fulfilling these desires. They create an image of how the future

116

should work out for them. But when it doesn't, they feel wretched. Such people are not only inherently dissatisfied with and plagued by boredom, they also rely entirely on hope.

> *"They strive to attain their prayers by every means, they teach and force themselves to do dishonorable and difficult things, and, when their effort is without reward, they are tortured by the fruitless disgrace and grieve, not because they wished for what was wrong, but because they wished in vain."*

Seneca, *De Tranquilitate Animi*, 2

We could say that *amor fati* – the practice of embracing fate – is a great antidote for those who rely on hope (for more see chapter 'Amor Fati'). Pursuing goals, whether long-term or short-term while embracing whatever the results may be, helps to focus on the present moment instead of worrying about the outcome, and being disappointed when the future doesn't bring us what we'd hoped for.

2) Being of service

Surprisingly, for some perhaps, Stoicism doesn't encourage people to shut themselves off from society. Instead, we should participate in humankind in a way that

117

fits us and benefits others. By putting ourselves out there to help our fellow human beings we kill two birds with one stone. Firstly, we put our minds at work by being busy with a certain task, and secondly, our readiness for service to others generates a sense of social connection, which simply feels great. Even though current society is totally different from society in those times, some values never change, being of service, for one. 'Being of service' boils down to taking a good look at ourselves, making an inventory of our skills, and seeing how we can use them to benefit humanity. Deriving meaning from your service is a road to fulfillment.

How does this lead to a calm mind? Well, by being focused on tasks, we are less likely to be distracted by things that don't matter to us in the last analysis. For example, I notice that when I'm fully immersed in creating YouTube-videos, there's no room for worrying about what's on the news or the negativity people have thrown at me in the past. Why should I? I'm doing something to entertain and benefit others; striving for excellence in work is only possible when residing in the present moment.

3) Choosing your friends wisely

"Nothing, however, gives the mind so much pleasure as fond and faithful friendship. What a blessing it is to have those to whose waiting

hearts every secret may be committed with safety, whose knowledge of you you fear less than your knowledge of yourself, whose conversation soothes your anxiety, whose opinion assists your decision, whose cheerfulness scatters your sorrow, the very sight of whom gives you joy!"

Seneca, *De Tranquilitate Animi*, 7

According to Seneca, friends can be a great addition to your life, but we should choose our company wisely. Some friendships simply revolve around negativity or are downright toxic. And, as we know, moods are contagious. A friend may be loyal and friendly, but when this friend is always upset and takes great pleasure in complaining about everything and harming us by our association with them, it's better to avoid that person. Instead, we might want to choose people that are, as far as possible, free from excessive selfishness, delusions, and vices. In other words, we should seek people that uplift us rather than burden us with their misery. So, how does this calm the mind? Well, a good and positive friend will not constantly burden us with all their issues and will assist us in achieving happiness. By avoiding negative friends, our inner peace will not be affected by their toxic behavior.

4) Not engaging in useless affairs

Seneca writes about how some people live their lives aimlessly, and spend their time going from place to place like ants crawling through bushes from twig to twig. We can see this happening a lot in today's day and age with more distractions than ever before. We go from our smartphone to our laptop, from Facebook to Instagram, and when we're halfway through a YouTube video, we're already bored and look for another stimulation. The key is to focus on one definite task, directing all our effort at that task, and only deviating from it when something important gets in our way. When working, for example, we could switch our phones to flight mode and turn off social media. We could also work according to daily schedules that provide us with clear objectives and directions so our focus remains fixed on that star in the sky, instead of lingering in limbo. At the end of the day, it all boils down to attention. The ability to pay attention makes all the difference between mediocrity and excellence.

5) Not depending on the opinions of others

Many people are constantly putting on a façade because they feel obliged to conform to the behaviors their surroundings impose on them. Seneca gives the example of a funeral, in which people may perceive it disgraceful not to weep when everyone is doing so. In such a case, we are expected to fake our grief even if, in reality, we don't have any desire to weep, but only do so to please people. This reminds me of the main character Meursault in Albert Camus' book *The Stranger*, who's repulsed by his own lack of emotions after his mother died. Seneca wrote:

> *"This evil of depending on the opinion of others has become so deeply implanted that even grief, the most natural thing in the world, becomes now a matter of pretense."*

Seneca, *De Tranquilitate Animi*, 15

When we depend on the opinions of others, we aren't free. It takes courage to free ourselves from this bondage, but when we do, we are truly brave because we take off our masks and show ourselves to the world in our purest form. Yes, we will be open to ridicule, but isn't it better to be ridiculed because of who we truly are, than tortured by perpetual pretense?

6) Balancing solitude and being in crowds

Seneca wrote that we should embrace both solitude as well as being in crowds. Solitude allows us to be able to withdraw into ourselves as well as long for company. At the same time, being in company makes us long for solitude. The one balances the other, and that's why the two things must be combined. Stoicism doesn't

121

encourage being a hermit but still does emphasize solitary activities like journaling and self-reflection. It doesn't deny that the mode of 'being alone' is part of life (see chapter 'Loneliness'). Solitude often charges our social battery after a period of socializing, while being in crowds grants us the joys and advantages of human connection. Socializing can be a great cure to relieve our minds from solitary ruminations as well. That's why many people feel revitalized after a bout of social interaction.

7) Giving the mind some relaxation (by drinking wine!)

Now, this is a tricky one – at least, the method that Seneca proposes. Seneca argues that the mind needs relaxation from time to time, and recommends washing away our sorrows and setting them free by the consumption of wine. Now, it's common knowledge that alcohol does a great job of temporarily making us happier and drowning our sorrows. Seneca does advocate moderation though. However, today we know that, for some people, moderation just isn't an option because there's an addictive element to their relationship with alcohol. Moreover, many people drink to get drunk. Didn't Seneca say that drunkenness is voluntary madness? But, at the end of the day, it could be beneficial for relaxing our minds without going to the extreme of intoxication.

Other avenues such as meditation practices, physical exercise, reading philosophical texts, or associating with tranquil friends and family members can have a very relaxing effect on the mind. However, if nothing of that works, getting drunk is indeed a way to forget the pain of life for a while. Unfortunately, this comes at a price.

Zeno

"We have two ears and one mouth, so we should listen more than we say."

Zeno of Citium

Zeno of Citium founded the Stoic school of philosophy around 300 BC,. He published a list of works on ethics, physics, logic, and other subjects, including his most famous work: *Zeno's Republic*, which *does* sound similar to a dialogue authored by Plato. However, despite Zeno being the founder of Stoicism and having written extensively, he is hardly cited in modern Stoic literature. The reason for this is simple: none of his works have survived! The good news is that other authors wrote *about* him. Biographer Diogenes Laërtius (not Diogenes the Cynic) preserved most details about his life, including a series of fragments that gives us an insight into what he taught.

There is no certainty about Zeno's ethnic and cultural background, except that his nickname was the 'Phoenician' and that Diogenes described him as a haggard, dark-skinned man. His father gave him books about Socrates he had brought back from his travels as a merchant. And, thus, Zeno became obsessed with philosophy. He became a pupil of the famous cynic Crates of Thebes, and among his other teachers were Polemo and

Stilpo. Later in life, Zeno started teaching himself in the *Stoa Poikile* (the Painted Colonnade) which became known as the home of Stoicism. His pupils were called Zenonians first, but later became known as the Stoics. Zeno was concerned with the whole spectrum of Stoic philosophy, from logic and epistemology to the nature of the universe which, in his view, primarily consists of matter and is governed by a divine principle. From this viewpoint, we could say that God doesn't exist apart from the universe: God *is* the universe. This is succinctly expressed in a quote by Zeno, preserved by the Roman philosopher Cicero:

> *"Nothing," he says, "that is inanimate and irrational can give birth to an animate and rational being; but the world gives birth to animate and rational beings; therefore the world is animate and rational."*

As quoted in *De Natura Deorum* by Cicero, 8.22

That's a weighty statement to ponder over. It lies at the basis of the Stoic belief, that the universe is governed by intelligent and primordial matter called 'Logos,' which can also be called 'Universal Reason' or 'Fate.' Living a life according to reason, therefore, is living a life in accordance with nature.

In regards to ethics, Zeno's view seems compatible with the later Stoic definitions of it. Simply put: 'virtue' is the only good, which has the end goal of a Stoic reaching a state of *eudaimonia* (see chapter 'Happiness'). In opposition to 'virtue' there is 'vice.' Zeno also laid the foundation for the system of indifferents, that is, things that aren't necessarily good or bad but can nevertheless contribute to self-preservation or destruction (see chapter 'Happiness'). He saw the human tendency for self-preservation as a part of human nature, which isn't virtuous on its own but could contribute towards one's efforts towards it. This set the Stoics apart from the Cynics, who rejected possessions and everything that satisfies the physical body. According to Stoicism, indifferents *do* have value, and we should pursue them, but not cling to them as possessions that will make our life better, but as a catalyst for living better lives in agreement with nature.

For example, wealth itself doesn't lead to virtue, but it *does* lead to self-preservation, which can *assist* in the pursuit of virtue. Another example: sickness doesn't lead to vice, but it is not a preferable thing because its destructive nature goes against self-preservation. Zeno also stated that 'bad feelings' are commotions of the mind, repugnant to reason, and against nature. So, even though emotions are part of our human nature, they are a sign of bad reasoning and could be overcome by getting a clear understanding of how life works. Grieving because of death could be overcome by accepting that death is a natural and inherent part of life. And our frustrations with 'bad parents' could be overcome by the knowledge that, at the end of the day, no one is entitled to 'good parents.' We see that all these misfortunes happen according to natural laws, which are, fundamentally, reasonable.

About Zeno's death, there is no consensus, as different sources tell different things. Also, our insight into Zeno's thoughts is very limited, because none of his works is extant. Some say that his contributions to Stoic philosophy, as we know it, were of high significance, while others believe that other philosophers like Cleanthes and Chrysippus were responsible for the actual development of Stoicism, and Zeno's role as 'founder' is more symbolic. Nonetheless, he remains a key figure in the history of Stoicism.

Stoic Exercises
for Inner Peace

Praemeditatio Malorum

─────────── ◦ઝᲢᲢᲢ◦ ───────────

The *praemeditatio malorum* can be translated as negative premeditation, and is commonly called 'negative visualization.' This is a popular exercise among modern-day Stoics. A maxim in the opening verse of the second book in Marcus Aurelius' work *Meditations* is the source of this idea. It goes like this:

> *"When you wake up in the morning, tell yourself: The people I deal with today will be meddling, ungrateful, arrogant, dishonest, jealous, and surly. They are like this because they can't tell good from evil."*

Marcus Aurelius, *Meditations*, 2.1

Now, the first part of this quote may come across as pessimistic. Aren't we supposed to be optimistic about the future and imagine that things work out in desirable ways? Well, not necessarily. People that are too optimistic often tend to deny the harsh realities of life. Denying them, won't make these realities magically disappear. Moreover, when they face them, they are disappointed that reality isn't as beautiful as they imagined. Despite the bleak outlook on the day ahead, Marcus Aurelius poses a realistic expectation, which is that when we go out in the world we'll indeed encounter nasty people at some point. So, wouldn't it be wise to prepare for these encounters?

Stoic philosopher Epictetus proposed a similar thought exercise that is less frequently presented as a model for the *praemeditatio malorum*. It goes like this:

> *"When you are going about any action, remind yourself what nature the action is. If you are going to bathe, picture to yourself the things which usually happen in the bath: some people splash the water, some push, some use abusive language, and others steal. Thus you will more safely go about this action if you say to yourself, "I will now go bathe, and keep my own mind in a state conformable to nature." And in the same manner with regard to every other action."*

Epictetus, *Enchiridion*, 4.

An essential part of the *praemeditatio malorum* is reminding ourselves of the nature of things. What's the nature of the action we're about to take? What's the nature of the objects or people we'll encounter? Marcus Aurelius reflects on this a bit further in the opening verses of the second book:

> *"But I have seen the beauty of good, and the ugliness of evil, and have recognized that the wrongdoer has a nature related to my own—not*

130

of the same blood or birth, but the same mind,
and possessing a share of the divine. And so,
none of them can hurt me. No one can implicate
me in ugliness. Nor can I feel angry at my
relative, or hate him."

Marcus Aurelius, *Meditations*, 2.1

In his memoirs, Marcus Aurelius keeps telling himself that we, as human beings, are here on earth to work together. We are part of a whole; everything is interwoven; all parts are connected, and our role is to live alongside each other in harmony. From this belief, he concludes that people that act against this premise – those who aren't virtuous and obstruct their fellow human beings and don't cooperate, act unnaturally. Marcus Aurelius argues that such behavior stems from ignorance of what is good and evil.

Unfortunately, we cannot change what other people think and do. But, with a little bit of compassion, we can contextualize their actions, and gain an understanding of why they behave as they do. Even though there's little we can do about people being meddling, ungrateful, arrogant, dishonest, jealous, and surly, there's at least one thing that's totally up to us: using our inner faculty. How do we approach difficult people? Do we meet them with anger or with compassion? First of all, there's no point in being angry at people that don't know any better. In this case, anger is just another

131

obstruction that is divisive rather than inclusive. Secondly, there's no point in being angry at nature. Nature is what it is, and being resentful about things that not only are beyond our control but natural as well, is pointless. What we can do instead is to accept the things that we cannot change and keep our faculties in a state of tranquility.

> *"For thus, if any hindrance arises in bathing, you will have it ready to say, "It was not only to bathe that I desired, but to keep my mind in a state conformable to nature. And I will not keep it if I am bothered at things that happen."*

Epictetus, *Enchiridion*, 4.

And so, the *praemeditatio malorum* can have the following benefits:

1) Coping

Preparing a situation in our minds allows us to find solutions beforehand, and visualize how we could handle the difficulties that may arise. This increases our ability to cope. We can contemplate minor difficulties, like being stuck in the traffic, but we may also want to meditate on certain tragic (but realistic) events like losing our loved ones or having a terminal illness.

2) Creating perspective

When we play out certain scenarios in our minds several times in a very conscious manner (and also reason them out) we put things in perspective. By changing our thoughts about events, we change the way they influence our moods. So, instead of seeing things as 'undesirable' and creating aversion towards them, we simply see them as part of nature. As Epictetus stated in the *Enchiridion*: "Don't demand that things happen as you wish, but wish that they happen as they do happen, and you will go on well."

3) Healthy detachment

By contemplating the impermanence of the things we love, for example, that we can lose our spouse today and that all our possessions can be taken away from us, we'll remain realistic about our relationship with them. As with everything, the people and objects we love are also part of the ever-changing whole, meaning that they will also cease to exist someday. We're no more entitled to our loved ones than a beggar is to a bucket of gold. As Epictetus argued: "Never say of anything, 'I have lost it.' but, 'I have returned it.'"

4)   Less 'shock'

The *praemeditatio malorum* is an anxiety reducer. Preparation means that we create order beforehand, so we become more resilient to the chaos that lies ahead. When we know and accept that a certain place is full of difficult people, for example, we'll be less 'shocked' if we were to actually encounter them. Whether or not something bad will happen is always uncertain. But, if it *does* happen, at least we are (mentally) prepared. We can overdo this, of course, and become obsessed by certain scenarios that might never happen, which will only lead to fear and anxiety. The *praemeditatio malorum* is not about harboring fear; it's about preempting fear in advance by rational thinking. The key is moderation and acceptance as opposed to obsession and resistance. So, by addressing possible future scenarios in a 'pessimistic' way, we not only set ourselves up for keeping calm in miserable circumstances, we also eradicate the possibility of disappointment and accept that everything in this universe comes and goes.

Mastering Self-Control

---------------- ꞉꞊꞉꞊꞉꞊꞉꞊꞉꞊ ----------------

The Stoics reiterate the theme of self-control regularly. Epictetus, for example, spoke about abstaining from talking about vulgar things; Marcus Aurelius pointed out that we should set limits to comfort and consumption, and Seneca saw people who have time for nothing but lust and wine as the worst types of all. Self-control means that we strengthen our inner faculty. A strong inner faculty ensures that we're less likely to be enslaved by outside forces that are not up to us. This means that impulses, triggers, and temptations have less power over us, which strengthens our position in an ever-changing universe.

This hit home when I fasted for seventy-two hours (meaning that I refrained from eating and only consumed water). The first day was the most difficult, but the second day was surprisingly easy – even blissful – and I was able to do all the tasks I normally do. This changed my perception in regards to food, as I used to think that I'd faint if I didn't eat for a day. After testing it out, it turned out that I was doing fine after a period of abstinence from food.

What I learned from fasting is that many of the desires that we may perceive as 'bodily needs' are created by ideas we have in regards to those desires. When we believe that we need a certain amount of food to still our hunger, we probably feel hungry if we don't reach that

135

amount, even if we're consistently overeating. Abstaining from food for some time can change one's relationship with it. I've become less prone to fear of not eating, knowing that I'll be fine and that I'm perfectly able to function when I don't eat for a while. As a consequence, I worry less about food. Nevertheless, it's always advisable to check with your doctor first before engaging in these kinds of experiments, as some medical conditions might not go well with fasting.

On the other hand, overindulgence comes at a price. We harm not only our bodies but also our minds if we fortify our attachment to satisfying the senses. The more we indulge, the more we'll need to indulge to experience gratification. The more we need gratification, the more we need to indulge. That's when people let their engagements in sensuality go out of hand as they're in constant pursuit of pleasure. They've become addicts, restless slaves to the sensory world.

The Stoics were aware of the dangers of sensual desires and concluded that, if we want to experience equanimity we should not pursue external pleasure. Marcus Aurelius called it "neither good nor useful." Seneca reflected on the festivities going on in the city, during which the Romans feasted, got drunk, and overindulged in pleasure. He argued that it's courageous to not participate in these festivities, however tempting. But it's even more courageous to participate but in a different way, namely, without extravagance. Because what a display of strength it is to be present among decadence and be able to restrain oneself. To detach ourselves from extravagance and test the constancy of the mind, Seneca gave us the following advice:

> *"Set aside a certain number of days, during which you shall be content with the scantiest and cheapest fare, with coarse and rough dress, saying to yourself the while: is this the condition that I feared?"*

Lucius Annaeus Seneca, *Moral Letters To Lucilius*, 18.5

Emperor Marcus Aurelius wrote that we should set limits on leisure time, emphasizing that we aren't made to spend our lives eating, drinking, and sleeping to excess. We'll notice that this is true when we observe many other living beings on the planet.

> *"Don't you see the plants, the birds, the ants and spiders and bees going about their individual tasks, putting the world in order, as best they can? And you're not willing to do your job as a human being? Why aren't you running to do what your nature demands?"*

Marcus Aurelius, *Meditations*, 5.1

137

There are many ways to train self-control. It all comes down to sense-restraint. A hyped term for a period of sense-restraint is the so-called 'dopamine detox.' During a dopamine detox, people refrain from activities that trigger the dopamine reward system for a certain amount of time. It's particularly aimed at addictive technology such as entertainment platforms, social media, smartphones, and the internet altogether. In our current age, we might want to restrict ourselves for periods from using these forms of technology so we weaken our addiction to them. Another simple method to train self-control is waiting a minute in front of your dish before you 'attack,' and then chewing on your food for a certain amount of time before swallowing. This is amazingly difficult for the untrained.

Self-control also makes us familiar with the hardship that many fellow human beings go through every day, like hunger, bad luck, and working insane hours without a vacation. Muslims, for example, fast during the Ramadan month partly out of compassion for those that are hungry. It also helps them to control the love of comfort and keep their desires in check. When we're more content with what we have and less dependent on what we think we need, we'll become less anxious about not getting what we want, or losing what isn't essential. As Seneca put it:

"Let us become intimate with poverty, so that Fortune may not catch us off our guard. We shall be rich with all the more comfort, if we once learn how far poverty is from being a burden."

Lucius Annaeus Seneca, *Moral Letters To Lucilius*, 18.8

How to Not Give a F***

Not everyone can appreciate swearing. But I believe that there's no better contemporary expression for being indifferent towards what people think about you than the words "I don't give a f***." Not giving a f*** isn't always a good idea. In many cases, it's much better and wiser to care. Not giving a f***, therefore, is a choice. It's a tool. And I'd like to share a Stoic perspective on the idea of not giving a f*** to explore optimal ways to practice it.

People generally over-inflate the importance of other people's opinions. There's clear evidence that the deep desire to fit in probably has its roots in the human survival instinct, as one's life in the distant past depended on the tribe. 'Fitting in' still has many benefits these days. In your teens and twenties, being a part of a certain group was a doorway to loads of fun, parties and, most importantly, opportunities to meet people of the desired sex. Few things change in adulthood, by the way, but after we've sowed our wild oats, and taken up more responsibilities, our priorities change. However, if we happen to be single as adults, having access to an extensive social life will grant us more dating opportunities.

Another benefit of being part of a group is that most of the time, we have a support network at our disposal that can assist us with many things. You can depend on them to be there for you – from practical stuff like moving to emotional care in times of hardship (in other words, providing our friends with material to gossip about). The downside of 'fitting in' is the price that comes with it. Being part of a group is often no free ride, as we're expected to attend parties and social gatherings, have friends over for a visit, and help them out when they're in need. Even though being part of a group can be a great thing, we don't need it for survival anymore in most of the developed Western world. Neither is it required to be liked by people we encounter on the street, or acquaintances we've connected with on social media. So, why should we worry any longer about what these people think about us?

From a Stoic perspective, the opinions of other people are not in our control. Things not in our control are seen as inferior to things that are in our control and are, therefore, unworthy of worrying about. A good reputation, as well as the ability to fit, can be categorized as a preferred indifferent (see chapter 'Happiness'): it's nice to be liked but not necessary to be happy. So it makes perfect sense to stop giving a f*** about things that are secondary that prevent us from acting from a place of courage, wisdom, moderation, and justice – the cardinal virtues in Stoicism. Epictetus stated that we should be willing to sacrifice our reputation to reach higher goals, like tranquility:

"You must watch, you must labor, you must get the better of certain appetites, must quit your acquaintance, be despised by your servant, be laughed at by those you meet; come off worse than others in everything, in magistracies, in honors, in courts of judicature. When you have considered all these things round, approach, if you please; if, by parting with them, you have a mind to purchase equanimity, freedom, and tranquility."

Epictetus, *Enchiridion*, 29

So, how can we care less about our reputations? How can we detach ourselves from the opinions of others? There are several exercises we can use to become more familiar with situations in which people judge us negatively and even socially ostracize us. The goal of these exercises is to build a first-hand experience that being disliked isn't the end of the world. Usually, this realization comes with age anyway. But if you're overly concerned about the opinions of others, it might be a good idea to give the exercises below a try. But be warned: these exercises could evoke some resistance from your surroundings (which means that you're doing a good job). It's like going to the gym; resistance is necessary for getting stronger.

142

1) Looking terrible in public

Most of the time when I'm out grocery shopping, I look like a homeless person because I am so casually dressed. Does this obstruct me from buying groceries? Not at all. Grocery shopping doesn't require people to look good, just acceptable enough to be granted entrance to the store. Now, the idea behind this exercise is that many people aren't comfortable going out without looking near-perfect. Some people spend hours in front of the mirror, just to go to the supermarket.

I won't deny that looking terrible can have consequences. Back in university I often attended classes wearing pajama-like sweatpants and flip flops. This outfit didn't keep me from studying and getting a diploma, but it could lead to people (like your professors) taking you less seriously, losing respect for you or even resenting you, which could obstruct your goals. Also, if you want to keep your job, this exercise is not recommended on the work floor. Even though the essence of this exercise is to devalue your reputation, it's just that you might want to choose your battles, and not ruin opportunities that rest on externals.

At the end of the day, this exercise teaches us that, in many cases, looking terrible in public isn't as bad as we believe. Sure, we might get some looks and giggles, but these don't hurt, now do they? The Cynic philosopher

Diogenes of Sinope used to sleep in a barrel on the streets, walking around in ragged clothes, 'pleasured' himself in public, and insulted people who walked past him. He didn't care what people thought of him. Therefore, no one was able to hurt him.

2) Saying 'no' to social events

Some people have such a fear of social abandonment that they're terrified of canceling social events in case people leave them. Yes, this happens sometimes. But most of the time it doesn't and the party is fine without them. And, if it *does* happen, well, it's not the end of the world (see chapter 'Loneliness'). The so-called 'fear of missing out' nonetheless deceives us into thinking that we must attend certain social events because, if we don't, we'll miss out on something essential. I've lost a close friend for repeatedly not showing up at his social events, including his thirtieth birthday party. However, even though this was very painful, it wasn't the end of the world. Friends come and go, parties come and go, and there will probably be plenty of opportunities to socialize as long as there are people. When we let the fear of abandonment rule our lives, we prevent ourselves from being tranquil. From a Stoic point of view, social events (especially those that revolve around pleasure) should be handled as secondary as they are inferior to the higher pursuits of virtue and equanimity.

3) Doing the opposite of what everyone else does

With being part of a group comes peer-pressure. We often see that people within a group tend to act in similar ways: they follow the same clothing style, share similar interests and views, talk the same way, hang out in certain places. If you're part of a group, a way to counterattack such herd behavior is doing the direct opposite. For example, if everyone wears sneakers, wear loafers. If everyone orders beer, order a soda. If everyone gossips about a particular person, don't participate; instead, change the subject. Gossiping is nasty behavior anyway, and Epictetus, who would agree, gives the following advice:

"If you are able, then, by your own conversation bring over that of your company to proper subjects; but, if you happen to be taken among strangers, be silent."

Epictetus, *Enchiridion*, 33

I've always been a non-conformist: hence the name Einzelgänger. Sometimes I was forced to because people didn't accept me. Sometimes I chose to deliberately. It's walking a solitary path in exchange for

145

not having to pay the price of conformity, which grants me a lot more freedom in many areas of life. Giving less f**** about a great many things saves energy and time to put in something more meaningful instead.

The Power of Journaling

Journaling is the habit of keeping a diary or log about our experiences, ideas, insights, and anything else that daily life evokes in our minds. The Stoics had a long-standing tradition of journaling, with Marcus Aurelius' *Meditations* as the clearest evidence. Marcus Aurelius never meant to publish his diaries, which makes it more plausible that the contents of his *Meditations* are his honest thoughts about a variety of topics. I could imagine that a man in the position of emperor and most powerful person in the world didn't have any equals to talk to, and thus resorted to pen and paper as an outlet. But could it also be that he was aware of the psychological benefits of journaling? Anyhow, his writings have provided humanity with profound wisdom to this day, and, thus, we could say that by journaling he built his personal Bible, which proved to be invaluable for many generations after him.

This brings me to the first benefit of journaling:

1) Preserving personal life lessons

It's great to have access to other people's experiences and learn about life by reading books or watching YouTube videos. But there's nothing like our own individual experiences. Every person is unique and so is every situation. And I believe that the only person we should compare ourselves with repeatedly when it comes to personal growth is our past self. By keeping track of our life lessons, we will know where and when *exactly* things went wrong and things went right. Why is this important? Many people make the same mistakes over and over again and just never seem to learn. By having certain key moments written down, it's easier to remember what we usually forget, so we can make wiser decisions in the present and future.

2) Illuminating what's in the dark

In Jungian psychology, the shadow is the realm in the unconscious that harbors unwanted personality aspects, thoughts, and desires. Because we all wear masks to show ourselves to society in a desirable manner, everything that's undesirable is kicked back into the shadow. But there's a lurking danger that the shadow will manifest itself in very destructive ways. Journaling is a way to make sense of our 'shadow behaviors' and keep track of when they emerge and what they look like. By doing this, we shine a light on our unconscious inner world and, bit by bit, we journal ourselves into our souls. This way of thinking isn't particularly Stoic, but I thought that it would be a nice addition.

3) Strengthening discipline

Keeping a daily journal is a discipline in its own right. That's why it's hard to stick to it. But, when we manage to write a journal every day, we'll affect other areas in life as well. Discipline is contagious. When I do something in a disciplined way, like physical exercise, I will automatically become more disciplined in regards to my nutrition and sleep, and let go of bad habits that obstruct the good ones. The effect of journaling is similar. Because, when I keep track of my activities, I'm more inclined to *do* these activities.

For example, one of my key habits is writing down my daily goals the night before. I make a note even if it's just one simple goal like writing a video script or doing the laundry. This helps me to stay disciplined the next day because my task is clear and the burden of the future limits itself to that task alone. This not only strengthens discipline but reduces anxiety.

4) Reducing anxiety

Writing down your thoughts brings relief. Life can be very chaotic and feed into destructive overthinking. Thinking, especially overthinking, is the cause of anxiety. Psychologist and researcher James Pennebaker of the University of Texas found that journaling removes emotional blockages and allows us to better grasp what's going on; this helps us to come to terms with stressful events. Simply put, journaling creates order out of chaos.

In a way, it's like cleaning a room. We take all the mess and put everything in order, remove the dust and make sure the place looks good. With journaling, we take the mess of our minds, put it into words, and remove the nonsense. This way, we *lose* our thoughts on paper, and save them for future consultation. We don't have to hold on to them anymore, which is a soothing idea. I usually save all creative thoughts and inspiration on my phone, so they're safe and won't linger in my head and clutter it unnecessarily.

After sharing these four benefits with you, here are some words of caution though. In an article in *Psychology Today,* Dr. Steven Stosny writes that journaling, when done wrong, can have negative effects on the mind. Journaling can make people self-obsessed, passive towards life (meaning: observing instead of taking action), wallowing in the past, going on and on about all the bad things that have happened to them. His advice on good journaling is, in a nutshell, doing it constructively, so it leads to solutions. Remembering how the ancient Stoics disapprove of ruminating about the past, I believe they would agree.

Memento Mori

Life is short. It's ticking away and seems to pass faster as we get older. Despite this, many people waste their lives on trivial pursuits. But there's an antidote. Thinking about death not only reminds us that we have a limited amount of time to do the things we want to do, it also teaches us to accept the reality of death itself and that it's all around us. *Memento mori* is Latin for 'remember thou art mortal.' In the famous painting *Vanité* by French painter Philippe de Champaigne we can see the three essentials of *memento mori*:

The hourglass stands for the notion that life is ticking away second by second. The rose stands for the truth about vitality, which is that, at some point, we all decay. The skull represents death. Today could be the last day you walk the earth. *"You could leave life right now. Let that determine what you do and say and think,"* wrote Marcus Aurelius. So, if you were to die today, what would you do?

Well, some people would certainly go on a hedonistic binge, obtaining whatever pleasure they can think of before they die. But, for those who follow Stoic principles, that wouldn't be a preferable option. They'd rather choose to spend their last hours as virtuously as possible, and take care of unfinished business as tomorrow would be too late for that. *Memento mori*, therefore, is a great antidote to one of the nastiest habits of mankind: procrastination. We encourage procrastination with the belief that we have an abundance of time. But when we take away that comfort, we'll face the necessity of doing our tasks as soon as possible, because tomorrow we might be dead. Thinking about death may evoke feelings of fear and sorrow. But this isn't caused by death itself but by our opinions about death. Here is a quote by Epictetus:

> *"Men are disturbed, not by things, but by the principles and notions which they form concerning things. Death, for instance, is not*

terrible, else it would have appeared so to
Socrates. But the terror consists in our notion of
death that it is terrible."

Epictetus, *Enchiridion*, 5.

When we stop fearing death and we see it as
nothing more than the insurmountable consequence of
life, we can be appreciative of the time that is given to us,
and not squander it doing petty things. Another dimension
of *memento mori* is preparation. Yes, we will lose the
people we love, sometimes in the most brutal of ways.
Just look at human history or look at what's happening in
the world right now: death is everywhere. Not being
affected by loss is, of course, easier said than done. Even
though the Stoics propose this ideal, most of us are still
human and have to deal with grief when someone we love
dies. Now, reminding ourselves of the possibility that we
can lose a loved one as we speak, helps us to be less
shocked when that happens.

For most people I know, losing someone they
love is excruciatingly painful. Humans are often so
attached to their loved ones that they cannot bear the loss.
But if we are mindful of the truth of death, we can
cultivate a healthier mindset towards the possibility of
loss. Instead of clinging to a person wishing that we would
never be separated, we could embrace the reality that the
day of separation will come. This doesn't mean that we
prohibit ourselves from grieving; it means that we were

prepared all along, which softens the blow. Because of this, we can be more functional and helpful human beings for the community when death occurs. In this case, losing someone due to mortality is mitigated. Here's how Marcus Aurelius puts it:

"Don't look down on death, but welcome it. It too is one of the things required by nature. Like youth and old age. Like growth and maturity. Like a new set of teeth, a beard, the first gray hair. Like sex and pregnancy and childbirth. Like all the other physical changes at each stage of life, our dissolution is no different."

Marcus Aurelius, *Meditations*, 9.3

What happens after we die? Will we enter the eternal nothingness that frees us of sense-perception, emotional turmoil, worry and rumination, and the enslavement of our bodies? Will we return to the flesh again for another cycle of life on Earth? Or will we enter another world for better or worse? No one knows for sure. But what we *do* know is that mortality is upon us. And when death smiles at us no matter where we go, is there a better response than to smile back?

The View from Above

────────────── ∘⅋⧲⊙⧳⅋∘ ──────────────

It's funny to look at ourselves and see how we quarrel about the smallest things, like the behavior of an annoying coworker during a meeting or the person who cuts us in traffic. From my own experience, it's very easy to get dragged along by a minor event, in a way that a dog is obsessed with a stick. We worry and fret about the future, and endlessly ruminate about the past. But, from a cosmic point of view, how significant are the things in which we invest so much emotional energy really?

Even though practicing Stoicism can be considered a very serious undertaking, there's also a sense of looseness in the words of Marcus Aurelius when he speaks of the insignificance of our lives concerning the bigger picture:

> *"The earth will cover us all, and then be transformed in turn, and that too will change, ad infinitum. And that as well, ad infinitum. Think about them: the waves of change and alteration, endlessly breaking. And see our brief mortality for what it is."*

Marcus Aurelius, *Meditations*, 9.28

In these eternal cycles of life and death, creation and recreation, we are even less than a grain of sand in the

Sahara desert compared to what we are in the universe. This doesn't diminish the fact that the human experience is intense and our senses are constantly tingling during our short lives on our tiny, blue planet. Sometimes we get so entangled in the human drama that we experience emotional disturbances like anger and anxiety. Some people are obsessed with wealth and fame, willing to make great sacrifices to get to the top, while, most likely, their names will be forgotten within a hundred years. And, even if we belong to the lucky few whose names will be preserved throughout the centuries, it's still insignificant when we look at it from a cosmic perspective.

Considering the entropic nature of the universe, the earth will disappear one day. If we don't destroy it ourselves, and the planet escapes the impact of a meteor, it will eventually be swallowed by the Sun when it enters the 'red giant phase' of its evolution. Who cares, then, how much money you hoarded in your savings account and who won the Nobel peace prize? Even the bloody wars we humans have engaged in will become insignificant.

> *"All things move in accord with their appointed times; they are destined to be born, to grow, and to be destroyed. The stars which you see moving above us, and this seemingly immovable earth to which we cling and on which we are set, will be consumed and will cease to exist."*

The idea of our comparative insignificance could lead some people to despair. But it could also be a very calming thought. The day-to-day problems that cause us so much headache, the constant striving for goals we deem utterly important, over-analyzing the past and future, obsessive thinking about what should be and should have been, what if we could view all this from a distance, and reduce it all to what it is: a mere dot in one of the countless galaxies in the universe? What foundation will be left for worry, greed, or anger?

The modern Stoics have turned the musings about humanity's place in the cosmos into an exercise called the *view from above*. This exercise gives us a temporary break from our daily affairs and puts them in another light. Changing our position towards external things changes the way we think about them which, in turn, changes how we feel. It's a Stoic form of meditation to calm the mind.

You start the view from above by visualizing yourself within your close and direct environment. It's like you are being watched through the lens of an advanced telescope that's placed thousands of light-years away. Imagine an alien civilization that's able to observe earth in real-time from a faraway solar system, looking at *you* sitting on a chair or lying in bed. Now, the telescope zooms out a little and focuses on your house. Then your neighborhood. You're already quite small in comparison

157

to all the streets and other houses. Now, it pulls out further and observes the city and its environment. See how small you are. It has become impossible to observe you with the naked eye. Then, compared to the vast area of land and water that surround it, the city has become nothing more than a small dot.

Consider the alien view of the continents on Earth spread across the globe, which predominantly consists of oceans that hold vast areas that we haven't visited yet. They see that Earth is only a small planet compared to other planets like Neptune or Jupiter, which, in their turn, are tiny compared to the sun. The sun isn't a big star compared to, let's say, Antares, which is eight hundred and fifty times its size. Both the Sun and Antares are part of the Milky Way which contains between a hundred and fifty to two hundred and fifty billion stars. When the aliens turn the telescope away from our galaxy and direct it outwards, it registers millions, even billions of other galaxies, many bigger than our own. Meditating on how small we are in the grand scheme of things, how short our lives are, and what we deem important matters less than we think, is both freeing and humbling.

Amor Fati

Earlier in this book, I've written about *amor fati* we translated as 'love of fate.' *Amor fati* is a concept in Stoic philosophy and is also used by existentialist philosopher Friedrich Nietzsche. The idea behind *amor fati* is to love and embrace whatever the outcome, no matter how hard we work towards certain goals. Being indifferent to the outcome enhances the ability to focus on the task at hand, and takes away the anxiety we may have. Simple as it is to fathom, implementing it isn't easy because most minds are hard-wired to spend time thinking and fantasizing about what might happen.

Being either harmed or delighted by certain outcomes is caused by desire and aversion. When we desire a certain outcome, we'll suffer when the outcome is different. When we're averse to a certain outcome, we'll also suffer when this outcome becomes a reality. So, by having strong desires and aversions, our happiness depends on what the future brings us. Sure, we're naturally inclined to desire things that are beneficial to us, like healthy nutrition and friendship (see chapter 'Aversion and desire'). But everything beyond the essentials isn't worth our pursuit to the extent that the idea of not attaining it causes anxiety.

The same goes for what we're averse to. Things like poverty, sickness, and having a bad reputation can be considered disadvantageous. But they're unworthy to worry about because these aren't the necessary ingredients for Stoic happiness. Still, many people are worried sick about the possible incurrence of something they're averse to, as well the possibility of missing out on what they desire. For them, 'embracing whatever happens' seems an impossible task, so they continue to live as slaves of Fortune.

Luckily, there are ways to train our inner faculty to become more at peace with the uncertainty of the future, more resilient to bad fortune, and simultaneously more indifferent to good fortune. Only then, can we embrace fate.

1) Purposefully exposing yourself to the thing you're averse to

The things we're averse to oftentimes aren't as bad as we imagine. It's very common among people to dread the idea of poverty, for example. With poverty, in this case, I don't necessarily mean the extreme poverty we can see in third world countries, but simply having just enough income to pay for the bare necessities like shelter, food, and clothing. In a wealthy country like the Netherlands being 'poor' means just that. In the modern capitalist world, we're bombarded with the idea that status and wealth are of utmost importance, and that 'poverty' should be avoided at all cost as it's portrayed as a hellish condition. But, at the same time, Buddhist monks take vows of poverty and let go of many sufferings that the rich and wealthy have despite their money, not to mention that many non-monastic people choose a low-cost minimalist lifestyle deliberately, and are doing perfectly fine. So, is this living condition that we call 'poverty' really that bad? There's one effective way to find out.

The key to reducing fear of certain outcomes is to expose ourselves to them, so we may experience that a perceived negative outcome isn't so bad. This way, we become familiar with hardship. So, when you fear poverty, how about living like a poor person for several days?

"It is precisely in times of immunity from care that the soul should toughen itself beforehand for occasions of greater stress, and it is while Fortune is kind that it should fortify itself against her violence."

Lucius Annaeus Seneca, *Letters to Lucilius,* 18.6

Another common fear is the fear of being single and alone (see chapter 'Loneliness'). When you're afraid of this, how about saying "No" to relationships for a season, and try to rely on yourself for happiness? Once we find out that being single can be a great thing, we are less likely to suffer from the fear of being alone once we're in a relationship again. This also prevents us from staying in abusive relationships, since we know that we can fend for ourselves.

2) Seeing any outcome as an opportunity

When I look back at my life, I've seen that many things that I feared did indeed come true. I've lost my job a couple of times, I've been kicked out of school, I've lost relationships, friends, and many opportunities. But on the flip side, I've gotten many other things in return, as life always tries to balance itself out. After I finished college, for example, I couldn't find a job partly because of the financial crisis back then. The worst scenario that I had painted in my mind came true: I had to work at several manual jobs that were way below my qualifications. When I look back, the experiences I had during these years were life-changing. Doing manual labor in factories and warehouses taught me how to work hard for little pay, created an opportunity to meet many great people, and also helped me to put things into perspective during the years to come: (1) that I'm able to do menial work if necessary (and can even have a pretty good time doing so) and (2) that I should be very grateful for the opportunity to earn more by sitting on my bum all day. So I was able to develop myself in certain ways that I would never have done had my life turned out as I had hoped.

I learned that every situation has something to teach. Even your worst scenario coming true can be a blessing in disguise. We may try so hard to avoid certain outcomes, but we truly don't know how they will affect our lives. In the same way, we don't know if the future we wish for will truly benefit us. So, I prefer to be open-minded about the future and to be receptive to what inevitably comes my way. Not *what* happens but *how we handle* what happens is what matters. Do we see the uncertainty of the future as an enemy to be feared, or as an opportunity to train ourselves to live well regardless of the circumstances?

> *"Don't demand that things happen as you wish, but wish that they happen as they do happen, and you will go on well."*

Epictetus, *Enchiridion*, 8.

3) Realizing that happiness is relative

In one of my earliest YouTube-videos, I discussed how happiness is adaptive. A study by Brickman, Coates, and Janoff-Bulman was conducted in 1978 to research the relativity of happiness. They studied a group of lottery winners, a group of paralyzed accident victims, and a control group, to determine which group was the happiest. We would expect that a lottery winner would be much happier than someone who ended up paralyzed as a result of an accident. We would also expect that those lottery winners would be much happier than the people in the control group that didn't win the lottery but weren't paralyzed either. In the first weeks or so, this hypothesis was indeed true. But a year later, the controls and the lottery winners were equally happy, and only slightly happier than the paralyzed accident victims.

After my uncle was diagnosed with terminal cancer, it surprised me how happy he was during the months before his death. I had never seen him that happy before. I'm glad that I had the opportunity to have a couple of long conversations with him, and he confirmed that he was indeed happy, grateful for the time he had left, and enjoying every minute of it. He rejoiced in seeing his grandchildren and gladly shared his insights with as many friends and family members as he could. For me, this was first-hand proof that, whatever tragedy or adverse circumstances, no matter how bleak, come our way, that won't exclude us from having a sense of happiness and wellbeing. With this in mind then, why should we fear adversity in the future? Spending so much time and energy doing so is probably worse than the future itself.

4) Being present

The ways I have listed so far have one thing in common: they point out that whatever happens, human beings find ways to cope with circumstances that are considered undesirable. Happiness is relative. So is unhappiness. The future isn't good or bad; it's just another path. Change is the very essence of life, and resisting change is like resisting life. It's the resistance to change that makes us suffer and not the change itself. As soon as we resist change, we're already in the future. Because instead of accepting the present moment, we try to preserve what has already passed for the days to come. Thus, we cling to the past and want to recreate it in the future.

But there's no future and there's no past. There's only *now*. When fate comes, it comes in the present. That's why embracing fate can only be done in the present moment. So, when the thing we anticipate hasn't happened yet, why worry about it? But when it comes, we might want to love it in the here and now – love it before it's gone. If we don't, we might regret that we didn't enjoy the moment when it was right before us.

And so, *amor fati* is the art of embracing whatever happens, and not needing a single day beyond the present. Epicurus, who was tortured by painful diseases, said: "Today and one other day have been the happiest of all!" In a way, he reminds me of my uncle. After more than a year of being consumed by a painful disease, he passed away with a smile on his face.